Rev. Charles R. Baxter

The
Making
of a
Christian
Leader

The Making of a Christian Leader

by
Ted W. Engstrom

Executive Vice-President
World Vision International

Foreword by W. Stanley Mooneyham

ZONDERVAN
PUBLISHING HOUSE
OF THE ZONDERVAN CORPORATION | GRAND RAPIDS. MICHIGAN 49506

THE MAKING OF A CHRISTIAN LEADER

Copyright © 1976 by The Zondervan Corporation
Grand Rapids, Michigan

Pyranee Books are published by Zondervan
Publishing House, 1415 Lake Drive, S.E.,
Grand Rapids, Michigan 49506

Library of Congress Cataloging in Publication Data

Engstrom, Theodore Wilhelm, 1916 —
  The making of a Christian leader.

  Bibliography: p.
  1. Christian leadership.   I. Title.
BV652.1.E53   254   76-13220

ISBN 0-310-24221-5

Printed in the United States of America

84 85 86 87 88 — 20 19 18

To
A few men, dear friends, among many,
who have modeled
Christian leadership for me –

Bob Cook, who taught me spiritual discipline

Ray Ortlund, my pastor, who has taught me what it means to love the brethren

Evon Hedley, who taught me loyalty

Stan Mooneyham, who taught me compassionate concern

Ed Dayton, who taught me how to plan better

Carlton Booth, who taught me the "Barnabas·principle" (the art of counseling)

Dick Halverson, who has taught me the real meaning of spiritual priorities

Pat Zondervan, who taught me the importance of detail

– and a host of unnamed other dear friends and colleagues who have ministered to me in their effective and varied leadership roles and styles.

Contents

Acknowledgment

I am immeasurably indebted to David J. Juroe for his excellent research and assistance in the preparation of this book. In his own right, David is a gifted author, successful pastor and Bible teacher, and Christian counselor. He has given of himself without reservation to help me in this task.

I warmly thank him — for without his deeply appreciated guidance this book probably would not have been brought to print.

TWE

Grateful acknowledgment is expressed for permission to quote from these publications:

Theological Dictionary of the New Testament, Vol. III, by Gerhard Kittel (Grand Rapids: Wm. B. Eerdmans Publishing Co., 1965). Used by permission.

The Art of Leadership by Ordway Tead. Copyright © 1963 by McGraw-Hill Book Company. Used with permission of McGraw-Hill Book Company.

Spiritual Leadership by J. Oswald Sanders. Copyright © 1967, Moody Press, Moody Bible Institute of Chicago. Used by permission.

Competent to Lead by Kenneth O. Gangel. Copyright © 1974, Moody Press, Moody Bible Institute of Chicago. Used by permission.

Excellence in Leadership by Frank Goble. Copyright © 1972 by American Management Association, Inc. Used by permission.

The Time Trap by R. Alec Mackenzie. Copyright © 1972 by Amacom, a division of American Management Associations. Used by permission.

Effective Psychology for Managers by M. M. Feinberg. Copyright © 1965 by Prentice-Hall, Inc. Published by Prentice-Hall, Inc., Englewood Cliffs, N.J. Used by permission.

Foreword

Where were you, Ted Engstrom, when I needed you?

What I would have given for a book like this when, fresh out of college, I was called to shepherd a little congregation in southern Oklahoma. Or, when at age 27, I was suddenly thrust once again into leadership waters far over my head. I had studied Bible. Had taken lots of courses in religious education. Had finally majored in religious journalism. None of which, I discovered, qualified me to lead a congregation or to be executive secretary of a denomination of 200,000 members.

Yet there I was, holding the title by virtue of an election at a church convention, and possessed with a strong urge to shout, "Help!"

Where were you, Ted?

I stumbled through. Struggled to stay afloat. Specialized in trial-and-error experiments. Made abundant mistakes.

I needed you then. I needed this book. Your advice and counsel would have been like a firm hand on my shoulder, a kindly voice in my ear saying, "Try this. It's a tested and proven principle of leadership."

But maybe you yourself didn't know the principles then. After all, you were still on the front edge of your own career — a career that would mark you as one of the most gifted and effective Christian leaders of our generation. How could either of us have known, or even guessed, that in the providence of God our paths would not only cross but merge and bring us together as teammates? Partners. In as exciting a Christian ministry as the last half of the twentieth century has seen.

Maybe you couldn't have written this book when I was struggling with my own leadership responsibilities. But now you can write it. You can be the firm hand and the kindly voice because you have lived what you have written. If anybody knows that, I do. Through our intimate daily association over seven years, I have watched those fantastic leadership qualities of yours mature and come to full fruit. I have been blessed by them. Benefited by them.

Now all those valid principles stated with such lucidity in this volume are weighted and warmed by your personality and experience. For me that's what makes the book so valuable. The book is you. Leadership problems are tackled, not in a vacuum, but in the crucible of personal encounter. That gives the book authority. These pages contain the distillation of your years in the publishing field, your strong leadership of the dynamic Youth for Christ movement, and your spectacularly successful years in management as executive vice-president of World Vision International.

The apex of your career is indeed an appropriate place from which to share something of what you have learned — of what you have been taught by life, by the Holy Spirit, by others. Just as I needed you then, an emerging generation of Christian leaders need now to hear the salutary word you say.

Sadly . . . tragically . . . the church has been so slow to train and qualify those on whom it has thrust leadership. Often we've thrown them into the deep waters of responsibility with little regard for instruction in the techniques and principles of not only staying afloat but, hopefully, inducing some forward motion. Your instructive and motivating book may well rescue the floundering and provide thrust for those who've been just treading water.

Oh, you and I both know that a single volume is not going to make a Christian leader. I remember a conversation I had a few years ago with a youthful friend of ours who had assumed the leadership of an organization with great potential. He asked me if I knew of an organization or school that was "turning out" Christian leaders. My answer was something like this: Nobody "turns out" Christian leaders. Certificates, degrees and diplomas don't make leaders. They can't be mass-produced like hothouse plants.

Rather, I said, they are like rare wildflowers, discovered growing sometimes in the least likely places. Fortunate is the movement or organization which, on finding such a promising example of the species, is able to transplant and cultivate it for maximum benefit and use.

Your book, Ted, is a part of the essential cultivation process — to change the metaphor — for many of us who feel ill-equipped or who need a refresher course to be all God wants us to be and all our responsibility demands us to be.

Now I know where you were when I needed you. God was fashioning you to be a leader so that you might be His instrument in the making of other leaders for our time.

Thank you, Ted.

And thank You, God.

—W. STANLEY MOONEYHAM
President
World Vision International

Introduction

O ur nation and world today are faced with problems that appear insurmountable. Security and defense problems are staggering. For the most part, our youth, our future leaders, are confused, alienated, and demoralized. Morals are at an all-time low. Moral standards are almost nonexistent. The growing national debt, bankrupt nations, financially troubled cities, and economic instability create more alarm each passing day. Amid these grave circumstances, our generation is facing an equally serious problem: a leadership crisis.

These crises, and many others, stem first from a lack of positive, constructive, dynamic, creative leadership. In some cases, no leadership is being exercised at all. Such crises of our time reflect a flight from the fundamental virtues and values which have made nations great. These values have been hammered out slowly through the centuries with great pain and sacrifice by strong and effective leaders. Many great civilizations down through the ages have abandoned these precepts. Those civilizations are known to us now only insofar as archaeologists can piece together their history by examining their ruins.

The successful organization has one major attribute that sets it apart from unsuccessful organizations: dynamic and effective leadership. Peter F. Drucker points out that managers (business leaders) are the basic and scarcest resource of any business enterprise.

The words of Karl Jaspers have an ominous ring for us today: "The power of leadership appears to be declining everywhere. More and more of the men we see coming to the top seem to be merely drifting." He further states that "the result is helplessness in a collective leadership that hides from the public."[1]

Many agree with his conclusions, pointing to the tragedies of pseudoleadership. It cannot be disputed that the success or failure, the rise and fall of groups, be they religious or secular, is determined by the quality of leadership. The only conclusion we can draw is that the need for dedicated and strong leadership is imperative.

In view of the grave threats to society there is an anguished cry for responsible leadership in the Christian world. It is not enough to rationalize that this is God's world and He'll take care of it, or that Christ is coming back soon, so what does it all matter anyway? Such cop-outs only compound the deepening problems and weaken the position of the Christian community that alone has the ingredients to upgrade and provide the adequate direction for a floundering generation.

Solid, dependable, loyal, strong leadership is one of the most desperate needs in America and in our world today. We see the tragedy of weak men in important places — little men in big jobs. Business, industry, government, labor, education, and the church are all starving for effective leadership. So today, perhaps more than ever before, there is such a need for leadership and teamwork to cope with the needs.

When we decry the scarcity of leadership talent in our society, we are not talking about a lack of people to fill administrative or executive positions; we have plenty of administrative "bodies." What we are deeply concerned about is a scarcity of those people who are willing to assume significant leadership roles in our society to get the job done effectively. The effective leader doesn't wait for things to happen; he helps make things happen. He takes the initiative.

National values as well as individual values are changing, creating gaps of communication and understanding, and generating feelings of frustration, anger, and insecurity on all sides. Today, with the requirement for leadership implicit in change, there are too few individuals with leadership qualities to manage the changes taking place.

Not only is there a great cry in our nation and world for political leaders who evidence integrity, but also the church desperately needs excellent, strong leadership. If this book contributes to the continuing attempt to define and stimulate people to step into the ranks of leadership, it will have served its purpose.

It should be stated here that whether we are talking about secular or church-related groups, the days of the ''self-made'' leader, the man who grows up with an organization and who knows it primarily on personal experience, are fast running out. Today's highly sophisticated organizations require leaders who have a thorough understanding of basic theoretic principles of management and human relations in order to accomplish success. This is not to infer that experience is unimportant, for leadership skills are developed and perfected only through practice. But the key is to know what to practice.

There is no shortage of literature and information to assist in developing leadership. The business world is deluged with material — so much so that the busy person is unable to sift through the volumes of advice. But this book is an attempt to better aid the Christian leader to identify basic principles and concepts to help him know what he is and what he must do. To that end, this book emphasizes not only management principles but those personal qualities and Christian virtues that will produce the best possible leaders for today and tomorrow.

It seems to many of us that Christian leaders, in the science of human relations, are oftentimes far behind our non-Christian friends who fulfill leadership roles in business, education, and the professions. Thus we need to explore areas of concern so that all Christian leaders can work together more harmoniously and effectively in the church and in other Christian organizations.

Christians have added problems and concerns because Christian organizations are different — or at least should be. They are different because they have a higher allegiance than the basic purpose of the organization. They operate on the assumption that they are doing something, are part of something, that has eternal value. They are different because the individuals in the organization share in the common allegiance to a ''God who is there.'' Because they have this higher and common purpose, they assume a moral and ethical level which should always transcend their short-range goals.

This means that Christian organizations must continually place a higher value on the worth of the individual and his personal development and needs. That is an easy statement to make, but in practice it discloses tremendous implications. When do we put the good of the organization above the immediate needs of the individual? How far can we go in letting the desperate plight of one member divert the group from its calling?

Furthermore, most Christian organizations have a degree of voluntarism to them. At one end of the scale is the organization that pays all its members a salary, but makes special demands on them because of this higher allegiance. At the other end is the local church, with very few, if any, paid workers. In this respect the local church is the most complicated and sophisticated organism in the world. It is one thing to lead a group of people who depend upon the organization for livelihood. It is quite another to motivate a group when 99 percent are volunteers!

This is precisely why we need to focus on leadership, for it is primarily up to the leaders to get any group or organization to function properly.

In the last several decades the institutional church has been maligned from both within and without. "Meanwhile," says Kenneth O. Gangel, "the barbarian society continues to paganize Western culture. The salt and light of Christ's disciples were never more needed. Someone has suggested that we live in a world 'come full cycle,' with society's norms reflecting a greater likeness to ancient Rome than those of any intervening civilization. The need for the church's life and ministry to touch the marketplace in Athens is apparent to all who care to notice."[2]

The many problems within the church and the short tenures of pastors and Christian workers testify to the inability of so much of present leadership to deal with the heavy struggles. This indicates that it is essential to have a clear concept of the nature of leadership, and to acquire this we borrow from secular research and analyze the Scriptures to formulate an adequate Christian philosophy — and theology, if you will — of leadership to guide Christian enterprises out of the morass.

To bring this down to where you live, are you a leader in a Christian organization or ministry that seems to be going nowhere? Are you frustrated by your inability to "get things moving"? There are pastors, denominational leaders, and executives in Christian organizations all over North America who are in the same plight.

Usually the problem narrows down to one significant factor, though there may be many different symptoms. An organization may have a fixed, grand objective — to serve Christ, to serve mankind, or to care for the needy — but too often that purpose is not stated in terms of what we intend to *do* to accomplish that purpose. The goals and objectives are not clearly defined.

A major sign of this malady is a large number of committees, departments, or boards that are organized around what they *do* rather than what *task* they are trying to complete. In the local church, for example, this might show itself in a multiplying number of Boards of Christian Education, Visitation Committees, Ushering Committees,

Building Committees, and various task forces. When these groups are formed, they usually have a clear idea of the why and the what. But after five, ten, or fifteen years their original goals become fuzzy, and institutional hardening of the arteries sets in. Each year new budgets are approved which are just an extension of "What we did last year, plus. . . ."

Staff are added to carry out this function or that. People are asked to "serve on this committee for three years." People are recruited less and less on the value of what is to be accomplished and more and more on allegiance to the organization ("after all, this is *our* church"). Sound familiar?

This book has been written to help the Christian leader to get a clearer picture of what he wants to *do* and *be* in a church or an organization, and how to get there. When I use the term *leader* in this book, I see him as one who guides and develops the activities of others and seeks to provide continual training and direction. This includes the president, administrator, executive, pastor, director, superintendent, supervisor, department head, and so on. It is a broader term than the popular term *manager*, which traditionally is associated more with industry or commerce.

Lawrence A. Appley, former president of the American Management Association, tells about writing a work that followed all the rules needed for a successful book: impressive title, research, and solid content that covered some fifteen years' experience. The book suffered, however, because it made a simple, natural process appear complicated and difficult. The result was that many readers did not finish the book and those who did were too confused by the apparent complexity of the subject to be able to profit from many of the good recommendations.

Much has been written about executive abilities, management policies, and leadership skills, and there have been so many arguments about whether leaders are born or made that the whole field of leadership has been engulfed in mysticism. As a result, many potential leaders develop fear complexes and imagine complicated situations where none exist.

The truth of the matter is that leadership is a perfectly natural status in life. The world is divided into leaders and followers. Civilization is bound to some kind of progress, and progress depends upon leadership. The process of natural selection, therefore, will generally provide leaders.

This book is written in the hope that the issue will not appear complicated, but that its content will quicken and challenge many to strive toward the higher qualities that go into better leadership.

One closing introductory word. This manuscript has been three years in the writing, but almost forty years in the making. I have been observing leaders, studying them, learning from them, and seeing what really makes them, for a good many years. Warm friendships have been formed with a host of Christian leaders. I have gotten close to them, observed them, been with them in innumerable situations. This learning process has been most meaningful, and I have become much the richer because of these associations. These men and women have genuinely ministered to me. Too often we forget that friends and colleagues with whom we work — as well as the very talents with which we identify ourselves and the abilities that we may have for leadership — are in themselves gifts from God.

I have discovered that the process of writing a book is infinitely more important than the book itself. In writing this book I found myself growing, analyzing, changing, synthesizing, struggling, and producing. The process itself is indeed the product.

Notes

[1] Karl Jaspers, *The Future of Mankind* (Chicago: The University of Chicago Press, 1963), p. 65.
[2] Kenneth O. Gangel, *Competent to Lead* (Chicago: Moody Press, 1974), p. 7.

The
Making
of a
Christian
Leader

CHAPTER ONE

What Is Leadership?

When God creates a leader, He gives him the capacity to make things happen.

A friend of mine once visited a friend of his in a little church in Connecticut. He had been there for many years, preaching to a handful of people. My friend said to him one day, when he saw the minister washing the church windows, "What in the world are you doing?" He was occupied with every menial task in the church — many tasks that could have been turned over to high-school students or men and women in the church. His answer appeared pious and commendable — actually it was tragic. He said, "I do everything myself [to demonstrate his self-sacrificing]. I run off my own bulletins. I wash the windows in the church, as you can see. I put out the hymnbooks. I do everything . . . this way I know it's done properly." Was that minister a leader in the best sense?

Well, what is leadership? Everyone knows what it is. Or do they? No one seems really to be sure. We are able to define what managers do, but the closest we seem able to come to a broadly acceptable definition of leadership is, it is what leaders do. Then when we try to define leaders, about all the agreement we get is that leaders lead.

Frankly, leadership is an elusive quality, if in fact it is a quality at all. Sociologists and psychologists have examined individuals for leadership traits, far too often with meager results. The fairly recent enthusiasm for group sociometrics has proved to be somewhat more rewarding, but still leaves much in doubt.

Why should we be concerned? Because, as stated in the preface, leadership development is the key to meaningful development of modern society and the effective future of the Christian church in the world. We must take a closer look, because true leadership is a quality found in far too few individuals.

Making Things Happen

Nicholas Murray Butler, a former president of Columbia University, said, "There are three kinds of people in the world — those who don't know what's happening, those who watch what's happening, and those who make things happen."

Though leadership may be hard to define, the one characteristic common to all leaders is the ability to make things happen — to act in order to help others work in an environment within which each individual serving under him finds himself encouraged and stimulated to a point where he is helped to realize his fullest potential to contribute meaningfully.

Outstanding results cannot be forced out of people. They occur only when individuals collaborate under a leader's stimulation and inspiration in striving toward a worthy common goal. Action is the key, because the leader and manager types are not mutually exclusive. The leader usually is a good manager, but a good manager is not necessarily a good leader because he may be weak in terms of motivating action in others.

When all the facts are in, swift and clear decision is a mark of true leadership. Leaders will resist the temptation to procrastinate in reaching a decision, and they will not vacillate after it has been made.

We might say, then, that leadership is an *act* or behavior required by a group to meet its goals, rather than a condition. It is an act by either word or deed to influence behavior toward a desired end. A leader usually leads in many directions. We often identify people as leaders by virtue of their occupying a position, possessing recognized skill, knowledge, or prestige, holding a certain social status, or having certain compelling personal characteristics. However, they still may not be included in our definition because of the inability to motivate people and act decisively to accomplish this. Complete is the man who can meet *every* act requirement in all situations. Few there are.

Never Passive Puppets

Men of faith have always been men of action. It is an impossibility for active men to serve in a passive role. This implies that such people are decisive in nature. Leadership action demands faith. The setting of and striving for goals is an act of faith.

Richard Wolfe in his excellent book, *Man at the Top,* points out that when God creates a leader he is given a volition for action. It is in this way that God works in people (Phil. 2:13). Wolfe further states that prayer is not a substitute for action which flows from decision.[1]

That Christ motivates leaders for action does not mean that human beings are merely passive puppets. This is unbiblical. Paul admitted that God worked in him (1 Cor. 15:10), but he never disclaimed his active part in getting results in his ministry. This is a part of the tension always evident in leadership action. The apostle was able toward the end of his life to say, "I have fought a good fight . . . " (2 Tim. 4:7), meaning that he recognized the need and effectiveness of grace, but he did not underestimate the attributes that made him an active agent in leadership.

PERFORMANCE TOO

For many years the World Olympic Committee has had to wrestle with Communist nations over their sending professional athletes to the Olympic games. Distinctions have been sharply drawn, especially by non-Communist countries. The basic difference between professionals and amateurs is that professionals earn their living or are paid.

We need to enlarge the definition of leadership to mean that professionals are also the best at what they do and get results. This means they are professionals because of their ability, not only to act, but to perform at a high efficiency level. Such would be true of all fields and vocations. Persons are where they are because of pre-scribed study and credentials. But more than that: they perform competently. If not, they soon lose their right to practice through competition.

FOR BEST RESULTS

If a leader is to act decisively to get results, he must follow certain principles. We will examine these in depth later on. But here are some of the major considerations to achieve the best results:

1. *Determining your objectives:* Determine the important end results you want to attain and when. State them in writing — accurately, briefly, and clearly.
2. *Planning necessary activities:* Decide what major activities must be performed in order to achieve your objectives: general objectives; specific objectives; long-range, intermediate, and immediate. Question every proposed activity:

Is it necessary? Is it important? Why?

3. *Organizing your program:* Make a checklist of all *important* things that must be done. Remember that urgent things are not necessarily important. Dwight D. Eisenhower said, "The important is seldom urgent, and the urgent is seldom important." Arrange these in an order of priorities. Make a breakdown of each activity. Identify essential steps in sequence of importance. Question every step: *What* is its purpose? *Why* is it necessary? *Where* should it be done? *When* should it be done? *Who* should do it? *How* should it be done?

4. *Preparing a timetable:* Prepare a work schedule. Set a time limit for the completion of each step in your program. Stick to your schedule — or reset it. Don't let time slip by without definite action. Follow through.

5. *Establishing control points:* Determine where and when you will review progress in relation to objectives. Establish bench marks. Make necessary adjustments. Determine remedial action as required.

6. *Clarifying responsibilities and accountability:* Clarify all delegated responsibilities, authorities, and relationships, and see to it that they are *coordinated and controlled.*

7. *Maintaining channels of communication:* Keep your associates (superiors, assistants, subordinates, and others affected) fully informed. Make it easy for them to keep you advised on all pertinent matters essential to successful operations.

8. *Developing cooperation:* Successful achievement largely depends upon groups of people working together. Clarify results to be accomplished; identify what is expected of every individual affected. Otherwise lost motion, misunderstandings, and frictions are almost certain to delay progress.

9. *Resolving problems:* Group thinking multiplies individual thinking and coordinates capacities of members of the group. Build morale through participation. An operating problem is any interference with desired end results.

   a. Spot the problem; clarify it. Tackle one specific problem at a time. Analyze underlying causes, contributing conditions.

   b. Develop possible solutions; select the best solution.

   c. Determine a plan of action; put it into effect.

   d. Check results in terms of improvements and objectives.

   Acquire: Explore: Sort: Assimilate: Utilize: Test: Act — Follow through.

10. *Giving credit where credit is due:* Recognize and give due acknowledgment and credit to all who assist in the successful attainment of your objectives. The *law of recognition* is as fundamental as the *law of action and reaction.*

There Is a Difference

Because leadership is an attitude as well as an action it must be distinguished from management. While there are certain functional similarities in both leadership and management, leadership has distinctive characteristics. It is unfortunate that so often little attention is given to these distinctives in developing organizational philosophy and in training an organization's executive personnel. Christian organizations are no exception.

What then are some of these distinctives? Comparison may be helpful at this point. My friend Olan Hendrix has made the following distinctions (with some personal modifications):

1. Leadership is a quality;
   management is a science and an art.
2. Leadership provides vision;
   management supplies realistic perspectives.
3. Leadership deals with concepts;
   management relates to functions.
4. Leadership exercises faith;
   management has to do with fact.
5. Leadership seeks for effectiveness;
   management strives for efficiency.
6. Leadership is an influence for good among potential resources;
   management is the coordination of available resources organized for maximum accomplishment.
7. Leadership provides direction;
   management is concerned about control.
8. Leadership thrives on finding opportunity;
   management succeeds on accomplishment.

Not So Easy

Sometimes one might see a leader effectively managing a group of people, and he is apt to think, "That looks easy. Let me at it. I can do that."

A friend of mine told me about friends who visited him in the East. My friend took two sons and two of his visitor's sons water-skiing. One was about fifteen years old; he said, "I'd like to ski too."

"Do you know how, Jim?"

"Oh, yeh, yeh, sure."

My friend agreed to let him try it. As the pilot pulled the rope taut, the boy's skis were very unsteady. When it seemed the boy was ready, the pilot raced the engine and began to pull the skis; legs and arms went all over the place! The pilot pulled back around, harnessed the boy again, and tried once more. Again legs and arms and skis went in all directions. After the fourth time my friend asked, "Jim, are you sure you know how to ski?"

"Sure, I know how to ski."

My friend thought better of the question and asked, "Jim, have you ever skied?"

"Well, maybe not, but it looks so easy."

That's the way it is with leaders. We stand a few feet back and watch a person leading effectively and think, "Oh, that's easy." So we smile, say a few words, write letters, and lead meetings. We can give orders and receive reports, and it's great . . . until we really try. Then we discover that the leadership function is not that simple. Most fail because they do not possess the inherent capacity to take the necessary and right actions.

To summarize, the concept of *leader* in this book means one who guides activities of others and who himself acts and performs to bring those activities about. He is capable of performing acts which will guide a group in achieving objectives. He takes the capacities of vision and faith, has the ability to be concerned and to comprehend, exercises action through effective and personal influence in the direction of an enterprise and the development of the potential into the practical and/or profitable means.

To accomplish this, a true leader must have a strong drive to take the initiative to act — a kind of initial stirring that causes people and an organization to use their best abilities to accomplish a desired end.

Notes

[1] Richard Wolfe, *Man at the Top* (Wheaton, Ill.: Tyndale House Publishers, 1969), p. 43.

CHAPTER TWO

The Old Testament and Leadership

> Moses chose able men out of all Israel, and made them heads over the people, rulers of thousands, of hundreds, of fifties, and of tens (Exodus 18:25).

C hristian leadership represents action, but it is also a set of tools for spiritual men. It is not moral or immoral — it is amoral. Effective leadership methods can be used for ulterior and worldly purposes by people who are not spiritual at all. By the same token, spiritual men can take these tools and use them for the glory of God, whether or not all the tools in the leader's arsenal are spiritual. The issue is the spirituality of the person and how he can better use leadership tools for the glory of God.

But where should the spiritual man look for the tools? Is it enough to borrow from the secular world and its literature?

A legitimate question may be asked, "Is the subject of leadership biblical? Are there valid principles for organization and spiritual leadership? Can we study the Bible and find methods to guide our thinking?" Yes, if we have an open mind to perceive its insights. I believe that every basic, honorable principle in leadership and management has its root and foundation in the Word of God.

GOD SEARCHED FOR LEADERS

The Bible is filled with examples of God's searching for leaders, and when they were found they were used to the full limit as they met His spiritual requirements, despite their human failings.

Close scrutiny of leaders mentioned in the Bible indicates most experienced failure at one time or another. Many failed at some point in their lives in a marked way, but the key to their success was that they never groveled in the dust. They learned from the hand of failure, repented, and then were used in even mightier ways.

Let us note several Old Testament passages. This is not intended to be exhaustive, but rather to stimulate the thoughtful person to further study and to gain insight into leadership excellence.

First consider Joseph. Is there in all of history a more magnificent example of leadership skill than his? Remember, he was placed in a high administrative position in Egypt not long after his jealous brothers had sold him to a passing caravan. He was given charge over the monumental harvest in Egypt. Then came the horrible years of famine, the delegation of the work, planning the whole operation, distribution of the materials, the foodstuffs, satisfying the complaints, and handling the grievances. The people he had to work with no doubt helped little (Gen. 41:14-57).

What a magnificent example of organization in Scripture! But God did not simply plant the skills in Joseph's brain so that he did it instinctively without thinking. I believe God does not work that way with men; generally I believe He will guide us to the subjects we need to study and learn if we show and exercise leadership qualities.

In the book I co-authored with my friend, Alec Mackenzie, *Managing Your Time,* I develop a biblical perspective regarding leadership.

> Any view of leadership must be based upon one's view of man. The Bible gives us a clear view of man: "All we like sheep have gone astray; we have turned every one to his own way . . ." (Isaiah 53:6). Thus, as sheep must be directed to move the entire flock along a single path, so groups of people need direction so that their efforts and energies will be directed toward a common goal.
>
> This direction which people need must come from the top. God has ordained this and Scripture teaches it in many ways. Moses set up lines of authority following Jethro's advice which we shall examine more closely (Exodus 18:13-27). The Aaronic priesthood was set up with a high priest and orders of priests under him in varying ranks (1 Chronicles 24). The husband is head of the home and a parallel relationship exists in the Church (1 Timothy 3:4-5). It is important to recognize that authority flows from the higher levels to the lower in God's plan.
>
> In Christian organizations there appears to be a recurring tendency to forget this. Confusing equality before the Lord with organizational equality, Christian workers may do themselves and their organizations

a great disservice by refusing to accept duly constituted authority. We are admonished, "Let every person be subject to the governing authorities" (Romans 13:1). We recall the Roman soldier who asked the Lord to come to his home to heal his servant, saying, "For I also am a man set under authority, having under me soldiers, and I say unto one, Go, and he goeth; and to another, Come, and he cometh; and to my servant, Do this, and he doeth it. When Jesus heard these things, he marvelled at him, and turned him about, and said unto the people that followed him, I say unto you, I have not found so great faith, no, not in Israel" (Luke 7:6-9).

PLACE FOR RESPONSIBLE AUTHORITY

None of this is to imply that all authority, of whatever character, is to be condoned. Authority carries with it great responsibility. Desirable authority is not viewed as being unwillingly imposed, all-powerful, insensitive and unenlightened. Those entrusted with authority are divinely ordained to use it responsibly for His purposes. His ultimate purposes and those of the organization — hopefully one — must be paramount. Sensitivity to the needs of those who are serving as well as those being served is essential.

The nature of authority may be far more complex than is commonly recognized even by those in management. The probability of this seems clear from the comment of Chester I. Barnard, the noted authority on management:

> A person can and will accept a communication as authoritative only when four conditions simultaneously obtain: (a) he can and does understand the communication; (b) at the time of his decision he believes that it is not inconsistent with the purpose of the organization; (c) at the time of his decision, he believes it to be compatible with his personal interest as a whole; and (d) he is able mentally and physically to comply with it.[1]

Barnard reminds us of not only the complex nature of authority, but also how much it does, in fact, depend upon the attitude with which it is received by those reporting to the person exercising it. Of the forces at work in leadership situations, we must identify those within the leader, those within the followers, and those within the situation. The life of Winston Churchill, who may not be seriously challenged for the title "Man of the Century," bears graphic evidence of these three kinds of forces. Recall that after marshaling the morale and the forces of the British Empire in her darkest hour during World War II, he was rejected by his own constituency and replaced as prime minister by Clement Atlee. He returned as prime minister at the age of 77, but never forgot the bitter lessons learned at the hands of fickle followers and history.

Then There Was Moses

Turning again to *Managing Your Time:*

The Bible has been quoted in numerous instances for its demonstration of management principles. One of the most outstanding examples is the instruction of Moses by Jethro some fifteen hundred years before the birth of Christ (Exodus 18:13-27). Noted below, from the Amplified Version, are these verses along with some of the management ideas and principles they suggest.

13. Next day Moses sat to judge the people, and the people stood around Moses from morning till evening.

(Observation and Personal Inspection)

14. When Moses' father-in-law saw all that he was doing for the people, he said, What is this that you do for the people? Why do you sit alone, and all the people stand around you from morning till evening?

(Questioning – Discerning Inquiry)

15. Moses said to his father-in-law, Because the people come to me to inquire of God.

16. When they have a dispute they come to me, and I judge between a man and his neighbor, and I make them know the statutes of God and His laws.

(Conflict Resolution Correction)

17. Moses' father-in-law said to him, The thing that you are doing is not good.

(Judgment)

18. You will surely wear out both yourself and this people with you, for the thing is too heavy for you; you are not able to perform it all by yourself.

(Evaluation – of Effect on Leader and People)

19. Listen now to me, I will counsel you, and God will be with you. You shall represent the people before God, bringing their cases to Him,

(Coaching – Counseling, Representation, Establishing Procedures)

20. Teaching them the decrees and laws, showing them the way they must walk, and the work they must do.

(Teaching, Demonstration, Job Specification, Delegation;

21. Moreover you shall choose able men from all the people, God-fearing men of truth, who hate unjust gain, and place them over thousands, hundreds, fifties, and tens, to be their rulers.

Selection, Establish Qualification, Assign Responsibilities.)

(Chain of Command)

22. And let them judge the people at all times; every great matter they shall bring to you, but every small matter they shall judge. So it will be easier for you, and they will bear the burden with you.

(Span of Control, Judging-Evaluation-Appraisal; Limits of Decision-Making; Management by Exception)

23. If you will do this, and God so commands you, you will be able to endure the strain, and all these people also will go to their tents in peace.

(Explanation of Benefits)

24. So Moses listened to and heeded the voice of his father-in-law, and did all that he had said.

(Listening, Implementation)

25. Moses chose able men out of all Israel, and made them heads over the people, rulers of thousands, of hundreds, of fifties, and of tens.

(Choosing-Selecting, Assign Responsibility, Span of Control)

26. And they judged the people at all times; the hard cases they brought to Moses, but every small matter they decided themselves.

(Judging-Evaluating, Management by Exception)

27. Then Moses let his father-in-law depart, and he went his way into his own land.[2]

PASSING THE TEST

It is clear from this passage that Moses received much direction and encouragement for the great tasks which lay before him. On numerous occasions he demonstrated great qualities of leadership even though his career as a statesman actually did not begin until he was eighty. At the outset, after God had called him, the people did not understand his role in their midst (cf. Acts 7:23-25).They asked, "Who made you a ruler and a judge over us?" Note that he never lost sight of his ambition and calling in life which made it possible for him to emancipate his people from the oppression of Egypt. His steadfast heart and consuming drive to achieve made him an outstanding example for all potential Christian leaders.

Moses' experience at the Red Sea showed how well he had passed the test for would-be leaders when he faced an utterly impossible situation. Who would not have shrunk from the task? Before him lay the Red Sea; behind, the legions of Pharaoh. The people, faced with certain annihilation, were complaining bitterly. But Moses, with a resolute spirit, focused on God's promises and exclaimed to the people, "Fear not." They all had every reason to fear. And because of Moses' faithfulness, God was able to demonstrate His power through one man, and it became a rallying point to assist the Israelites in their march toward the Promised Land. Superb leadership and implicit faith had won the day!

Later in the wilderness Moses had the right attitude, when he knew it was time to train someone else for leadership. He was fearful of being a paternal leader and pleaded with God to give the Israelites a successor. Thus, he did not indulge in self-pity, knowing that he would not lead the people into the land of promise. He was more concerned about the right kind of direction and future leadership.

WELL SPOKEN OF

The New Testament provides a rather comprehensive commentary on the outstanding leadership qualities that Moses possessed, enabling him to succeed (Heb. 11).

1. Faith (v. 24: "By faith Moses, when he was come to years, refused to be called the son of Pharaoh's daughter.")

2. Integrity (v. 25: "Choosing rather to suffer affliction with the people of God, than to enjoy the pleasures of sin for a season.")

3. Vision (v. 26: "Esteeming the reproach of Christ greater riches than the treasure in Egypt: for he had respect unto the recompence of the reward.")

4. Decisiveness (v. 27: "By faith he forsook Egypt, not fearing the wrath of the king: for he endured, as seeing him who is invisible.")

5. Obedience (v. 28: "Through faith he kept the passover, and the sprinkling of blood, lest he that destroyed the firstborn should touch them.")

6. Responsibility (v. 29: "By faith they passed through the Red Sea as by dry land: which the Egyptians assaying to do were drowned.")

It is no wonder that to this day, nearly all Jews — Orthodox, Reformed, and Conservative — consider Moses the greatest of all the prophets and leaders in the long history of Israel.

A STRONG SPIRITUAL LEADER

David, the second king of Israel, was a striking contrast to Saul, the first king. Whereas David was noble, generous, and admirable, Saul was ignoble and lacked most of the fine qualities one expects in leadership.

David came to the throne about 1000 B.C. and reigned for approximately forty years. He conducted many wars of conquest, laid the foundation of the Solomonic empire, and initiated a period of splendor and power for the Israelite nation that has never been equaled. Behind David's accomplishments was the blessing of God. The reasons for his success are not difficult to find.

When David was approached by the elders of Israel (2 Sam. 5:1-3) they recognized his many sterling qualities and strong traits of leadership.

The nation had been torn by civil war, and the people were weary of strife. The happiness and prosperity of Judah under David motivated the rest of the tribes to desire the administration of David's kingship.

But in addition, the relation of all the tribes to David was an inducement: "We are thy bone and thy flesh." They would have him know that their feelings toward him were warm and tender. David was no foreigner, unqualified by the Mosaic law to be king over the Lord's people (Deut. 17:15).

The Israelite tribes through their representatives advanced another good reason for desiring David as their king. They referred to his former valuable service to the nation: "When Saul was king over us, thou wast he that leddest out and broughtest in Israel."

They were telling David that he was the real power in Saul's government. Saul was only a figurehead. It was David who led Israel against their enemies and returned with the spoils of victory. Who then was more qualified to fill the vacant throne?

The strongest reason of all that the Israelite tribes offered for wanting David to rule was that he was God's choice. "The Lord said to thee, Thou shalt feed my people Israel." Christian leaders serve better when they are convinced they are in the will of God, for then they know they will be equipped for their tasks by God's power.

As a leader, David possessed qualities which attracted others. The elders came to him (2 Sam. 5:3a); he did not go to them. He had ruled Judah well for seven years, and there was every reason to believe he would rule all the tribes as well. David took a loyalty oath with the people to protect them as their judge in peace and their captain in war. They in turn obliged themselves to loyalty and obedience to David as their sovereign under God. Such a sacred pact and solemn inauguration inspired much confidence in the people.

Valiant conquest and wise administration were important elements in the glory of David's reign. His very first exploit after he became king over all Israel was to capture Jerusalem from the Jebusites and make it the capital of the twelve tribes. He showed his valor by storming and taking the city. He displayed his political and administrative sagacity as well when he made the city the capital. Jerusalem was not so centrally located as Shechem, but he must have thought through the decision well. Jerusalem was a natural fortress, and it had a high elevation on the central highland ridge in Palestine that made the city a delightfully cool spot through the torrid summer.

SECRETS TO DAVID'S SUCCESS

There were several secrets to the glory of David's leadership. First, wise diplomacy distinguished his reign (2 Sam. 5:11). The king's generosity and attractive traits of personality won him many allies. He knew how to placate enemies as well as win friends. He was lovable. He made friends readily, while Saul had the strange ability to alienate people. These traits made David a successful diplomat. Those who did not respond to his generous nature he dealt with by force. But the wise, like Hiram of Tyre, cultivated his friendship and sent representatives to offer him favors.

Hiram I of Tyre (c. 969-936 B.C.) was a contemporary of both David and Solomon. He presided over a commercial kingdom with his capital in Tyre. His people dealt mainly in commerce and were skilled artisans, shipbuilders, and technicians. Hiram had access to the Lebanon forest of cedar in Syria and helped David with skilled labor and building materials for the construction of a palace and, doubtless, other major construction projects.

Thus we see David possessing the ability to reach out and strategically build his own empire. Leaders must have this quality — to treat and lead others in such a way that their contributions may be used to good advantage.

Second, David's recognition of the Lord God in all his blessings made his rule outstanding (2 Sam. 5:12). He did not take credit to himself for all his success and prosperity. He was not boastful and self-assuming, as are so many who become power hungry. He humbly attributed his rise to power to the Lord and saw Israel as the Lord's people and himself as the leader under God, responsible to the Lord for leadership. Christian leaders who would lead people in this manner need never worry about success. When they recognize their highest responsibility is to the Lord, it makes all the difference in the world.

Third, David constantly sought the Lord's blessing (2 Sam. 6:12-15). This is the occasion of the ark's being brought to Jerusalem. There had been an earlier attempt to get the ark, but a Levite named Uzzah put out his hand to support the ark in defiance to a command of the law (Num. 4:15).

The ark was left in the care of Obed-edom the Gittite. Those who watched the ark saw that the entire household of Obed-edom was blessed because of its presence in his house. They told David the news. When David heard it he proceeded to bring the ark into the city.

He knew the absolute necessity of having God's blessing upon his work and administration. The Christian leader today needs no less desire for his life and work.

Fourth, as a leader David was not ashamed to be involved in spiritual exercises. He was able to acknowledge the need for sacrifice for sin (2 Sam. 6:13). This time every precaution was taken to insure the proper conduct of the ark to the city. He rectified the former mistake. He did not place the ark in a cart now, but ordered those whose business it was to carry it on their shoulders to do so.

At the outset, when the Levites "had gone six paces," David offered sacrifices of "oxen and fatlings" as atonement for former errors. When the Levites finished their task in safety, a thank offering of seven bullocks and seven rams was brought (1 Chron. 15:26).

David was also unashamed to praise and thank the Lord (2 Sam. 6:14). He "danced before the Lord with all his might." He leaped for joy because his heart was so filled with gladness, and he was so taken up with the Lord's glory that he became almost oblivious of the fact that he was, after all, a dignified king. This more than anything else gives us insight into the heart of a man who loved the Lord so much that he did not concern himself about what people thought.

Lastly David, as a strong leader, led his people in praising the Lord (2 Sam. 6:15). The great king thought it no disparagement to his dignity to lay aside his royal purple and put on the simple garb (a linen ephod) in order to minister better to his people. Such a garb was used in religious exercises by those who were not priests, as in the case of Samuel (1 Sam. 2:18).

The result was that the people brought the ark to Jerusalem with loud acclamations; they were demonstrative and joyful. They brought the ark to the city of David and put it in the place that the king had provided (cf. 1 Chron. 15:1; 16:1). In the presence of the ark, God was in the midst of His people.

David illustrated clearly that the Christian leader, too, must be willing to exercise spiritual means to mold, stimulate, and continually challenge his colleagues and subordinates. In spiritual work we rather expect it; in the secular world many shy away from it. However, the principles abide: God will always bless those who highly regard Him, no matter what the endeavor.

A LEADER OF LEADERS

A striking example of strong leadership is Nehemiah, who along with Ezra and Zerubbabel was instrumental in rebuilding Jerusalem's temple and wall. Talk about organization! He possessed many qualities prerequisite for leadership excellence. His character was beyond reproach; he was a praying man; he displayed great courage in the face of much opposition; he had a deep concern for his people exhibited by his insight, tact, impartiality, and decisiveness. Furthermore, he did not shirk responsibility given to him.

Nehemiah had a tremendous ability to encourage his country-men and then express appreciation when it was in order. He quickly dealt with problems before they became too severe. Thus he was a strong leader who was able to inspire his people to great heights.

His organizational ability, disclosed by his skillful strategy and detailed plans, is a challenge to every would-be leader. Read the entire Book of Nehemiah, looking for every leadership and management principle.

The books of Ezra and Nehemiah tell of the returning exiles from Babylon and how they were absorbed into the Jewish community at the time. The accounts are a grand illustration of the importance of planning. Ezra stated that in all, 42,360 exiles returned with 7,337 slaves and 200 singing men and women. The priests numbered 4,289, there were 74 Levites, 128 singers of the children of Asaph, 139 porters, and 392 Nethinim and children of Solomon's servants.

COMPLETE REORGANIZATION

At this time some of the social and religious traditions were changed, especially in music. During the days of reconstruction there were more singing guilds, and the temple ministry was reorganized. The musical staff was enlarged (1 Chron. 6:33-37). Details are preserved of the organization of the Levites as well as the porters who were distributed among the different gates. The Levites were divided into various areas of responsibility such as work in the chambers and the treasuries (cf. 1 Chron. 9:26-32; 23:24-32). These accounts were no doubt referring to the period of Nehemiah.

THREE FACTS STAND OUT

In summarizing this great leader, we can say that Nehemiah is known in Bible history as the great builder. In Nehemiah 3:1—6:16 three facts stand out. We see how great he was as an administrator. He knew what he wanted to do, how it had to be done, and who was to do it. The what, how, and who are tremendously important. They spell the difference between success and failure. Nehemiah had a clear objective or goal, a sound technique, and a good enlistment program. His function as an administrator included the ability to *analyze*.

He also succeeded in a program of total mobilization after he determined the plan. Everyone in and about Jerusalem was involved, from the high priest and his fellow priests to the goldsmith and the merchants (Neh. 3:1-31). The two rulers of Jerusalem as well as the common citizens were involved. At first some nobles did not feel it was proper for them to do such work, but apparently they changed their minds (cf. 3:5; 4:14). Thus Nehemiah mobilized the entire population, revealing his ability to *deputize* and *delegate*.

Finally we see how Nehemiah achieved perfect coordination. In Nehemiah 3 it is almost tedious to read the phrase "next unto him (or them)." It appears over a dozen times, and "after him" another dozen or more times. Every man had his work and his place. Such perfect coordination enabled the wall to be finished in record time. We clearly see Nehemiah's ability to *supervise*.

Indeed, Nehemiah stands forever as a model for all would-be leaders who aspire to the heights of success, because he organized the whole nation and fulfilled his role as leader.

GOD ORDAINS MEN TO LEAD

The ancient Wisdom Literature of the Israelites, such as Psalms and Proverbs, addresses itself a great deal to leadership principles. One of the Proverbs says that the hand of the diligent shall rule. The *Living Bible* reads, "Work hard and become a leader" (Prov. 12:24). A true leader will use his imagination to improve his work and anticipate the next task.

That God ordains men to serve is clear from Psalm 75:6,7: "Promotion cometh neither from the east, nor from the west, nor from the south. But God . . . putteth down one, and setteth up another."

The Bible constantly discloses the fact that God searches for men whom He can count on as leaders. Note the following examples:

1. 1 Sam. 13:14: "The Lord hath sought him a man after his own heart."

2. Jer. 4:25: "I beheld, and lo, there was no man."

3. Jer. 5:1: "Run ye to and fro through the streets of Jerusalem, and see . . . if ye can find a man . . . that executeth judgment, that seeketh the truth; and I will pardon it."

God's plea for stable and effective leadership is probably best epitomized by the prophet Ezekiel, who said, "I sought for a man . . . that should . . . stand in the gap" (Ezek. 22:30).

Notes

[1] Ted W. Engstrom and R. Alec Mackenzie, *Managing Your Time* (Grand Rapids: Zondervan Publishing House, 1974), pp. 87-89.

[2] Ibid., pp. 89-91.

CHAPTER THREE

Christ and Leadership in the Gospels

Christ's method of leadership sets the example: "The Son of man did not come to be served but to serve . . ." (Mark 10:45).

A ny study of Christian leadership is incomplete unless the life of Christ is studied. It is essential to recognize at the outset that He epitomized the concept of leadership by His own statement: "The Son of man did not come to be served but to serve; . . . I am among you as one who serves" (Mark 10:45; Luke 22:27 MLB).

If Christ spent so much time with the disciples, it is certain that He wished to impress them with the example of His life. He came to serve, and so should they. This was His method of leadership. He unselfishly gave of His life, which culminated in His death on the Cross. The Old Testament predicted the Messiah would be a "suffering servant." His service did not degenerate into servility; He was humble, but retained dignity.

His kind of service set an example. He was willing to wash His disciples' feet. His perfect, sinless, human life ended in self-sacrifice at Calvary. Thus He showed His followers how to serve, and He demanded no less of those who would carry on His work on earth. Jesus teaches all leaders for all time that greatness is not found in rank or position but in *service*. He makes it clear that true leadership is grounded in love which must issue in service.

When we take a closer look at His earthly service, we discover that His ministry was mainly teaching. He spoke with authority. At times the greatest learned men of the synagogue were startled by His teaching. He knew that the only way to perpetuate truth was to pass it on, so He set out to train His disciples.

Furthermore His leadership demanded that others be obedient. He did not want His disciples to use their position for selfish purposes. So His leadership was largely carried out through teaching and training as well as through keen interest in individuals and their problems.

Another major consideration is that Christ's service was redemptive. He came to provide freedom for man: "The truth shall make you free" (John 8:32). This idea must dominate the relationship between any true leader and the group. There must be a dynamic, living relationship — that is what is meant by *redemptive*. Men who had faith in Christ not only found eternal life, but were changed in the here and now. The Christian leader, following the pattern of Christ, will not use the group to achieve his own ends without regard for people who constitute the group. He will want to allow people to be themselves and thus be liberated. It is not a slavish conformity to the group that he seeks, but to help people serve a cause with joy, commitment, and a motivation that is prompted by Christ Himself.

CHRIST AND AMBITION

All Christians live under the mandate to develop their lives to their utmost. The apostle Peter urged us to "grow in grace, and in the knowledge of our Lord and Saviour Jesus Christ." This calls for sanctified ambition, with a strong drive to forge ahead and achieve. For centuries Christian mystics and others have written and spoken disparagingly of ambition, in the ordinary sense of the word, thinking it to be sinful.

However, ambition when used to the glory of God is praiseworthy. The word comes from the Latin which means "canvassing for promotion." It is true that men can have much selfish ambition to control others, enjoy power for power's sake, and be unscrupulous in money-making and the control of other people. But Jesus gave to the disciples a different standard of ambition and greatness. "But Jesus called them to him, and saith unto them, Ye know that they which are accounted to rule over the Gentiles exercise lordship over them; and their great ones exercise authority upon them. But so shall it not be among you: but whosoever will be great among you, shall be your minister; and whosoever of you will be the chiefest, shall be servant of all" (Mark 10:42-44).

This passage reveals the true nature of ambition for a Christian leader. It is not to be according to worldly standards where men seek gain. Ambition is to be clothed with humility. It is not the number of one's servants that count, but the number whom one serves. Greatness of exaltation is in proportion to greatness of service humbly rendered. True greatness, true leadership is achieved in selfless service to others. This is the clear teaching of our Lord. History and the contemporary scene are replete with those who have exemplified this selfless service: Florence Nightingale, Mother Teresa of Calcutta, Sadhu Sundar Singh, Watchman Nee, Martin Luther King, Ken Taylor — a contemporary who has contributed all profits from the printing of the *Living Bible* into a charitable foundation — and so many, many more.

My good friend, Kenneth O. Gangel, who has stimulated my thinking about leadership, has made a vital contribution to the understanding of this biblical concept in his outstanding work, *Competent to Lead*. He has already done the major research in aptly setting forth both the positive and negative aspects of New Testament leadership. The remainder of this chapter and part of the next are adapted from his book as we consider this important theme (cf. *Competent to Lead*, pp. 11-16, used by permission).

WHAT LEADERSHIP IS NOT

Biblical leadership in terms of Christ's life is also clearly seen when we consider the negative side of the question.

A marvelous passage in Luke 22 holds some valuable principles for helping us analyze our Lord's view of leadership. The passage itself is contained in verses 24 through 27, but the context is of great importance also. The Lord had just ministered to the disciples in the final supper together in the upper room. They had finished sharing the bread and the cup and had experienced among themselves a worship relationship of the highest order, with the incarnate God in their midst and with the Father in heaven. It is almost unbelievable that the scene recorded in these verses could have followed that experience.

1. *New Testament leadership is not political power-play.* Immediately after sharing the symbolical representation of Christ's flesh and blood, the Scriptures record that the disciples fell into a dispute. The word is *philoneikia* and literally means "rivalry." What is even more interesting is that this word does not describe an accidental falling into argument on occasion, but rather the possession of a habitual contentious spirit. To put it another way, because of their fondness for strife, the disciples verbally attacked one another in an attempt to gain political prominence in what they expected would be

an immediately forthcoming earthly kingdom. Martin Buber once said that persons' inability to "carry on authentic dialog with one another is the most acute symptom of the pathology of our time."

Political power-play in the church is even more reprehensible than it is in the world. Yet it is striking that even before the first church was organized at Jerusalem; before a pastor ever candidated for appointment to a congregation; before an official board ever met to design a building program, the church knew how to be contentious! Toward the end of the first century, John bemoaned that in at least one church there was a man named Diotrephes who liked "to have the preeminence among them," and the Diotrephesian tribe has multiplied in nineteen hundred years of history.

2. *New Testament leadership is not authoritarian attitude.* Luke 22:25 records our Lord's reaction to the arguments of His disciples. He offered first a comparison and then a contrast. The comparison is that their behavior at that moment was like the behavior of the Hellenistic monarchs who ruled in Egypt and Syria. Their leadership style is described as "exercising lordship" — the word *kurieuo*, which appears frequently in the pages of the New Testament. At times it is used to describe the authority of God (Rom. 14:9). Paul used the word often to refer to a negative control, such as death's attempt to hold dominion over Christ (Rom. 6:9); the power of sin in the life of the believer (Rom. 6:14); and the hold of the law on men freed by the gospel (Rom. 7:1).

A similar word (*katakurieuo*) is used to describe Gentile rulers; the control of demons over men (Acts 19:16); and as a negative example in describing the behavior of elders with saints in the church (1 Peter 5:3). The verb form is never used positively of Christian leadership. To put it simply, *Christian leadership is not authoritarian control over the minds and behavior of other people.* Peter remembered the lesson of this night, for in writing his epistle he warned the elders not to "lord it over God's heritage."

The first part of Luke 22:26 has a grammatical construction of strong contrast: "but ye, not so." The kings of the Gentiles wished to be called "benefactor" for any little deed of kindness they might show to their subjects; it was expected they would practice autocracy and demagoguery. Whether that is right or wrong is not the issue; the point is that *Christian* leadership is *not* that kind of authoritarian control. Indeed, in defiance of that culture, our Lord added that one who is greatest in the church is actually *as* the younger, and the "boss" (leader) is *as* the worker.

3. *New Testament leadership is not cultic control.* One of the beautiful words in the work of the church is *diakanos*. It means

"service" and is precisely what Christ did for His disciples in that upper room. The questions of verse 27 seem to be rhetorical: who is more important, the waiter or the dinner guest? Obvious answer: the dinner guest of course! But who is the guest and who is the waiter at this Last Supper? Answer: "I am among you as he that serveth."

Conclusion: *New Testament leadership is not flashy public relations and platform personality, but humble service to the group. The work of God is to be carried on by spiritual power, not personal* magnetism, as Paul clearly pointed out in 1 Corinthians 1:26-31. Some leaders may *serve* the Word, and some leaders may *serve* tables, but all leaders *serve* (Acts 6).

The positive pattern of Christ in developing leadership in His disciples is clearly enunciated in A. B. Bruce's helpful book, *The Training of the Twelve.*[1] He suggested that the total report of the Gospels covers only thirty-three or thirty-four days of our Lord's three-and-one-half-year ministry, and John records only eighteen days. What did Christ do the rest of the time? The clear implication of the Scriptures is that He was training leaders. What kind of leaders? How did He deal with them? What were the important principles of His leadership development program? Although it is not the purpose of this book to deal with the total subject of leadership development, certain principles may be helpful in making a transition to a positive declaration of what New Testament leadership is.

THE POSITIVE SIDE

Dr. Gangel suggests four positive declarations of what the leadership of Christ was like:

1. The leadership of our Lord focused on individuals. His personal conversation with Peter, recorded in John 21, is a good example of the way He gave Himself to His men in an attempt to build His life and ministry into them.

2. The leadership of our Lord focused on the Scriptures. His treatment of God's absolute truth was not diluted by relativistic philosophy. It held the Old Testament in highest esteem. The rabbis had distorted God's revelation, and the Leader of leaders now came to say, "You have heard that it was said, . . . but I say to you" (Mt. 5:21-48).

3. The leadership of our Lord focused on Himself. Remember, in John 14:9, how he found it necessary to say to one of the disciples, "Philip, have you been so long with Me and you still have not known the Father? Take a good look at Me because if you

understand Me you understand the Father'' (author's paraphrase).

4. The leadership of our Lord focused on purpose. Christ had clear-cut goals for His earthly ministry, and a limited time in which to achieve them. If you knew you had to leave your present ministry within three-and-one-half years and turn it over completely to subordinates you would be allowed to develop during that period of time, how would you go about doing it? You could do no better than follow the example of Jesus, and the result would probably be a great deal like the leadership that characterized the New Testament church.[2]

Notes

[1] A. B. Bruce, *The Training of the Twelve* (New York: Harper, 1886).

[2] Kenneth O. Gangel, *Competent to Lead* (Chicago: Moody Press, 1974), p. 14.

CHAPTER FOUR

The Epistles and Leadership

A leader is like a father who nurtures his children through exhortation and encouragement.

There is a temptation, when dealing with the issue of New Testament leadership, to turn to the Book of Acts because of its vivid description of early church life. It does provide a pattern for church government that is normative for church organization even though it is highly undeveloped. Among the vital lessons to be learned and taught, the book discloses the necessity of Christians to work together.

It is interesting to note that Christ did not reveal a complete church order, ready-made, when He gave the keys of the kingdom to Peter and the other apostles. The structure of the New Testament church unfolded as the church applied itself to its task through the leadership of committed men. There were the formation of missionary teams, the gathering together of workers in various groupings, the utilization of house-churches as well as the development of city churches, and the diversification of forms of Christian service. Sound leadership was required.

We are told in Acts that the Christians of that era turned the world upside down for Christ. This was not done by random and haphazard preaching of the gospel by a few vigorous men. It took much planning and strategy to effectively reach that generation.

But for a biblical study of leadership the Book of Acts is insufficient by itself, because it is primarily a historical narrative, not a developed ecclesiology. We will be better helped by looking at the epistles of Paul and Peter, who apparently were commissioned by the Spirit of God to organize local churches and to speak God's plan and pattern for the functioning of those churches. A passage in 1 Thessalonians 2 will serve as a model.

New Testament Church Leadership Is Nurture

Nurture is a botanical term which describes the care and feeding of a young plant so that it grows properly to maturity. In 1 Thessalonians 2:7,8 Paul used some distinctive words to describe what nurture really is in the eyeball-to-eyeball relationships that mark leadership responsibility. He speaks of being "gentle" — the word *ēpioi,* used often of a teacher who is patient in the nurturing process of seemingly incorrigible students. In 2 Timothy 2:24 Paul used the word to describe "the servant of the Lord." As if that emphasis weren't enough, he referred to the gentleness of a "nurse," which is an obvious reference to a nursing mother, not a hired baby-sitter. The word is used in the Old Testament to describe Jehovah's care of Israel.

But there is more to this emphasis on nurture. A gentle nursing mother "cherishes her children." The word is *thalpē,* which literally means "to soften by heat" or "to keep warm." Deuteronomy 22:6 in the Septuagint uses the word to describe a bird caring for its young by spreading its feathers over them in the nest. Such a nurse is "affectionately desirous" of the growing children, a term that seems cumbersome but appears in the Thessalonians passage in the AV, ASV, and RSV texts. The implication is a "yearning after" for the good of the group, which ultimately, as verse 8 indicates, results in a sacrifice on the part of the leader.

Where is the manliness in all this? Where is the image of the sharp voice barking orders and "running a tight ship"? Where do we see the legendary Marine sergeant? Again a pagan culture distorts our understanding of spiritual reality. We identify masculinity with toughness and ruggedness, but God identifies it with tenderness. We think of leadership as "handling" adults, but God thinks of it as nurturing children. Joyce Landorf's book addressed to husbands is so appropriately entitled *Tough and Tender.*[1]

New Testament Leadership Is Example

The hard work of Paul's leadership spills out in 1 Thessalonians 2:9. During both day and night with great effort he worked among the believers. His life and his colleagues' lives were examples of holiness, justice, and blamelessness before God. Note that this was behavior *before the believers,* not an attempt at evangelism. In 2:5,6 Paul assured the Thessalonians that their leaders were "men," not some kind of superhuman ecclesiastical giants who wanted to run the organization by sheer executive skill and personal power.

NEW TESTAMENT LEADERSHIP IS FATHERHOOD

What does a father do? According to Ephesians 6:4 he is responsible for the nurture of children. Consequently the model of the family is used to describe not only regeneration in terms of infant birth, but also leadership functions as the teaching role of a father in the home. The words rendered "exhorted and encouraged" in 1 Thessalonians 2:11 are the words *parakalountes* and *paramuthoumenoi.* These are commonly used together in Paul's writing. The former is often used of divine ministry, but the latter is always a human word. It is *never used directly for God's comfort, but rather is descriptive of the way He uses people to minister to other people in the community of faith.*

A father also "charges" his children. The word has the idea of admonishing or witnessing truth so that they walk in patterns acceptable to God. I can think of many who have ministered to me so effectively and personally in the "father" role — men like Paul Rees, Carlton Booth, the late Jacob Stam, Herbert J. Taylor, and others. How we should thank God for those who have modeled this role in our lives!

Earlier we noted the positive pattern of Christ in leadership training. Now we mention the example of the apostle Paul. The development of the New Testament church is the multiplication of the lives of the few people described in Acts 1. Many early church leaders were personally trained by Paul; he was, in effect, the "pilot project." Timothy, Silas, Titus, Epaphroditus, the Ephesian elders, and many others grew out of his life and ministry.

There are local churches today which look much like the worldly leadership condemned by our Lord in Luke 22. If we are to serve our own generation with power and effectiveness, we must stop pretending that being a Christian leader is like being a king of the Gentiles.[2]

PAUL'S WORDS TO TIMOTHY

A key passage stating the qualifications of leaders is 1 Timothy 3:1-7. This is a crucial passage on church government. It deals with a man who was a bishop, an overseer. Two terms are used for church leaders in this text: *elder* and *presbyter.* These terms are applicable to the same person, as borne out by such passages as Acts 20:17 and 28 (cf. also Titus 1:5-9).

Two legitimate questions may be asked. First, if they were one and the same person, why were different terms used? Most modern scholarship concludes that there is little difference in the terms. It could be pointed out that *presbyteros,* the elder, describes the leaders as they personally were; they were the older, more respected men. *Episkopos,* the bishop, the overseer, describes the function and task; a bishop was to superintend the church.

Second, if the elder and bishop were the same, how did the bishop become what he did become? The answer is that as the early church grew, it became essential for a leader to emerge from the elders. The elder who arose became known as the overseer.

Several factors produce this kind of thinking. For example, in Titus 1:5 we are told that the ministers were to appoint elders everywhere; this was clearly done in the church wherever they went. In Acts 14:23 we are told that after the first missionary journey, Paul and Barnabas appointed elders wherever there was a church.

Then we find that the qualifications of the two are really for all purposes identical. Titus 1:5 says, "For this reason I left you in Crete, that you might set right what was defective and finish what was left undone, and that you might appoint elders and set them over the churches in every city as I directed you" (*Amplified*). Paul when speaking of elders in the middle of the passage changed the term and called them bishops or overseers (1:7). The qualifications of 1 Timothy 3 and Titus 1 thus appear to be identical.

Again, after his third missionary journey, Paul called upon the elders of Ephesus to meet him at Miletus (Acts 20:17), and in verse 28 he referred to them as overseers. So the same title may be applied to both elder and bishop.

Then the question may be asked, "How did the term *bishop* come to be used?" It is a truism that wherever you have a body of people together, some will emerge as leaders. They will evolve naturally. So from these elders emerged some leaders, and they became known as bishops. They were then ordained or set apart, to be ministers or leaders of local flocks.

A LONG HISTORY

The institution of elder had a long history even preceding the constituted church. We get the word *Presbyterian* from the Greek word; today a church by that name is built around a court of elders. In Numbers 11:16 we read of the appointment of seventy elders to help Moses in the administration of the people: "And the Lord said unto

Moses, Gather unto me seventy men of the elders of Israel, whom thou knowest to be the elders of the people, and officers over them; and bring them unto the tabernacle of the congregation, that they may stand there with thee."

Now, there were elders even before they were appointed. They were the officers to guide the Israelites. The Holy Spirit was not revealed at that time to all believers, but He came upon individuals one at a time for a unique ministry. To this day every orthodox synagogue has its elders who are recognized as the spiritual leaders in the community. In the formation of a synagogue, ten men, called a *minyan,* were required to initiate a formal congregation. They were usually strong community leaders. What a help it would be if we Protestants had more community leaders to serve also as leaders in the local congregation.

These elders or *presbyteroi* were respected, fatherly figures used by the Lord to give direction to the church.

The second term in 1 Timothy 3, *episkopos,* gives us the English word "Episcopalian." It is translated "overseer" or "superintendent." This concept also has a long and honorable history. In the Septuagint this word is found several times. In 2 Chronicles 34:17 there is a description of the men who were overseers of the public works projects. The Greek translation from the Hebrew used the word of those who were sent out to establish new colonies. It is a picture of an individual who has the oversight of something. In the New Testament it would be a person who has the oversight of a church or a group of churches.

SET APART

Before we briefly study their major qualifications, it is to be noted that New Testament leaders were formally set apart for their office. They were ordained (Titus 1:5). The elders were given honor and duly recognized. They had to undergo a time of testing to prove themselves (1 Tim. 3:10). They were paid for their work (1 Tim. 5:18). They were liable to censure (1 Tim. 5:19-22). The tenor of these passages discloses that they were not novices.

Paul saw their duty as being not only to the church, but in other areas also. If they failed there, Paul said, chances were strong that they would also fail in the church. The first was the elder's duty in his home: a man who could not properly instruct his own household, Paul reasoned, would not be able to train a church. The second concern was the bishop's responsibility in the world: he must have "a good report from them who are without" (1 Tim. 3:7). He must be respected in the day-to-day living beyond the four walls of the church. That is the real test. Few things have hurt the church more through the centuries than leaders who have failed in their societal obligations.

Paul developed other key qualifications in 1 Timothy 3:1ff. First, he said, the Christian leader must be a man "against whom no criticism can be made" (*anepileptos*). This word is used of a position which is not open to attack. It is an extremely high standard, for this person must be free not only from definite civil charges, but must also be beyond criticism. In this life, of course, no man can fully attain such a position, but it is an ideal that we must expect to be more nearly met in true leadership.

Second, the leader must "have been married only once." Several interpretations grow out of this text. But in the context we may be quite certain that it means he is a loyal husband, preserving his marriage vows and the sanctity of the Christian home. He must be able to manage his household well. As is obvious from the rest of the New Testament, this does not mean how well he can dictate and control his family, but rather how well he has developed the relationships within his family that are Christ-honoring and people-honoring.

Next, the Christian leader must be "sober" (*nēphalios*), and a few verses later he is told not to overindulge in wine. The word *paroinos* means to be addicted to wine. *Nēphalios* also mean "watchful" and "vigilant"; *paroinos* also means "quarrelsome" and "violent." So the burden of the passage is that the leader must not allow himself any indulgence that would soil his Christian witness.

Then Paul used two words to describe two more essential qualities for the Christian leader: *sōphron*, translated "prudent"; and *kosmios*, translated "well-behaved."

The word *prudent* is translatable a number of ways, including possessing a sound mind, discreet, chaste, and having control over sensual desires. In biblical times a person having this quality was considered self-controlled. Spiritually, in this kind of a person Christ reigns supreme.

The well-behaved leader is so because he is *sōphron* in his inner life. *Kosmios* means externally orderly and honest. So a leader's passion must be in control, and outwardly he must have recognized beauty.

A leader must also be hospitable. Much stress is found in the New Testament on this theme. The word *philoxenos* contains the idea of one who keeps an open heart and an open house; he does so without grudge. In the early church there were wandering teachers and preachers who needed homes to stay in. The true leader is sensitive to those in need.

Next, the Christian leader must have an aptitude to teach (*didak-*

tikos), says Paul. Instruction is a vital part of any meaningful and successful enterprise.

The Christian leader must not be a striker *(plēktēs).* The individual is not to assault others when they err, but tries to be reconciled with those with whom he disagrees.

Gentleness is another important characteristic. The word is *epieikēs,* and it is difficult to translate literally. In classical Greek it connotes the quality of correcting the law when the law appears to be unjust. A true leader, then, is one who knows when to retreat from the rigid, unjust letter of the law and can apply it with a right spirit. It could also include the notion that a leader should remember good rather than evil.

Two final thoughts remain in this passage. First, the Christian leader must be peaceable *(amachos).* He knows how to achieve ends through tranquil means rather than by bullying people. He also must be free from the love of money *(aphilarguros);* he measures achievement of both himself and his subordinates without continually attaching a dollar bill or self-enhancement. His perception is more in terms of the intrinsic value of people and labor.

These qualities outlined by Paul were recognized even in the pagan world. William Barclay quotes an ancient writer who once described an ideal commander: "He must be prudent, self-controlled, sober, frugal, enduring in toil, intelligent, without love of money, neither young nor old, if possible the father of a family, able to speak competently, and of good reputation."[3] How much more does God expect of His children who are leaders!

PETER SPEAKS UP

The apostle Peter speaks to the issue of Christian leadership in his first epistle (1 Peter 5:1-7). When he wrote this letter he was a prominent figure in the early church. Besides being very close to Jesus, he became honored and respected because of his vital role in the formation of the first church at Jerusalem. It was he who preached a mighty sermon the very day the Holy Spirit was revealed to believers at Pentecost (Acts 2).

Thus it is important to hear his advice. Few passages show the significance of Christian leadership more clearly than 1 Peter 5. The writer began by addressing his words to his fellow elders; he set down the perils and privileges of leadership. First, Peter said, leaders are to care for the flock. They are to be properly motivated — not by coercion, but out of willingness. He will accept his responsibility, not merely out of duty, but with real compassion for others.

Second, Peter pointed out the high calling of leadership. A man must be interested in more than making a shameful profit, so that he will not be affected in his task or decisions by any personal gain that is unbecoming his office. Next, a leader is not to be dictatorial, a petty tyrant; his major consideration is to be a worthy example for his flock. He is not driven by the love of power or authority.

Humility, said Peter, should be shown in his relations with others, but he must also be challenged to react humbly to the testings that God allows in his life. "Allow yourselves to be humbled" would be close to the text (v. 5).

Finally, the true Christian leader will not resist or rebel against the experiences of life, but will accept God's hand upon his life. He will be aware that God is molding him more like His Son through trial. Through suffering God can settle a man as well as restore one who has been trusting in his own flesh.

These qualities are essential if a leader is to serve effectively.

Notes

[1] Old Tappan, N. J.: Fleming H. Revell, 1975.

[2] The preceding pages of this chapter are adapted from *Competent to Lead* by Kenneth O. Gangel (Chicago: Moody Press, 1974), pp. 14-17.

[3] William Barclay, *The Letters to Timothy, Titus, Philemon* (Edinburgh: Saint Andrew Press, 1962), pp. 86-87.

CHAPTER FIVE

Administration
Is a Gift

> Where no wise administration exists, the people will floun-
> der (Prov. 11:14).

In the body of Christ today, the world over, there
is a much-needed renewed emphasis upon the study of
spiritual gifts, often to the exclusion of other vitally important doc-
trines. However, it is a subject we should not neglect, because the
calling of men by God is a major theme in the Bible. He is a living
God who addresses His Word to man. He does not speak to all men
only in generalities, but often calls men by name into service. The
apostle Paul recognized his own gifts by insisting that he would not
glory beyond his measure (2 Cor. 10:13). He would not seek to enter
into a sphere of service for which he was not qualified by the gifts that
constituted his own calling. On the other hand, the gifts that he
received made him a debtor to discharge them (cf. 1 Cor. 9:16,17;
Rom. 1:14).

It is clear that one of the gifts God metes out to men is a special
ability to administer or manage. The same Paul, for example, spoke
of those who have the unique ability to administer in governmental
affairs.

In the listing of gifts of the Spirit in Romans 12, Paul mentioned
gifts of teaching and exhorting, but also the gift of diligence to qualify
the man who governs. This concept of the administrative exercise of
government by leaders in no way contradicts the organic form estab-

lished by the gifts of the Spirit. It is only the recognition that among the differing gifts there must be those to help people to work together by providing adequate organization and direction.

In the Old Testament is an outstanding illustration of a man with the gift of administration. That is Solomon, who devised well-laid plans to build the temple and make Israel a solid economic power. The temple plans are spelled out in detail in 1 Kings 5—7.

As a part of the whole plan, Solomon devised a method to divide the land into districts for tax revenue to support the government's efforts to strengthen the nation's economy. He did not follow the pattern set forth when the land was split up along tribal lines after the Israelites first entered Canaan. The plan was so efficient that the indescribably beautiful temple was completed in record time, and it remained the spiritual center of the people for centuries. Solomon evidenced a real gift to administer the plan and make it effective to obtain a positive result.

Because his successors could not follow Solomon's plan and maintain the nation's unity, the kingdom became fragmented into party rivalries and eventually split into the southern kingdom (Judah) and the northern (Israel). The kings who ruled after him did not have the gift to administer or organize the people consistently.

When some Christians look at Solomon and others in government or business administration, whether stated or implied, they consider these distasteful or a secondary gift, appearing less important than other functions of service. Frequently one hears pastors consider these areas to be nonessential, uninteresting, and less spiritual than, say, preaching, teaching, or counseling. For centuries the church, beginning with the rise of monasticism, has drawn a sharp distinction between what is sacred and what is secular. This is unfortunate. People who reason this way misunderstand a significant biblical concept that sets forth the function of administration as a cherished spiritual gift.

The Greek word commonly translated "minister" or "ministration" is *hupēretēs*. The noun form appears only a few times. The verb "to minister" appears numerous times. It is also translated "to serve." The Greek word is a compound: *hupo* meaning "under" and *eretēs* meaning a "rower." So the basic concept behind the word is literally a person who "steers or rows a boat." The word also appears in the Septuagint, which is the Greek translation of the Old Testament.

Let us examine some of the main passages in which the term is used.

In Luke 4:20 the word signifies the attendant at a synagogue service. The apostle Mark is called an attendant or minister in Acts 13:5. Paul is considered a minister in Acts 26:26, as also in 1 Corinthians 4:1, where he is associated with others such as Apollos and Cephas as "ministers of Christ."

Another word used interchangeably in the New Testament is *kubernēsis,* which also refers to a person who guides a ship. This word is found only three times. The "helmsman," mentioned first in Acts 27:11, had a great responsibility to guide the ship through an imminent storm which Paul, a prisoner, had predicted. The ship administrator had to know in those days all about navigation and significant information to get the ship to its destination.

The second instance, found in Revelation 18:17, closely parallels the Acts reference in meaning. Here the writer, the apostle John, reviewed the great wealth of Babylon as viewed by commercial men and "every shipmaster." An important distinction should be made. The helmsman was not some ordinary seaman who followed orders, but he was engaged by a shipowner, along with the rest of the crew, who were the shipmaster's subordinates.[1] Therefore he was the responsible person aboard, the leader or captain of the ship.

The third reference is the most important for our studies in Christian leadership because it appears in the passage that delineates spiritual gifts (1 Cor. 12). In verse 28 Paul clearly disclosed that administration is a distinct gift. The King James Version translates the word "governments," but the word *administration* best fits the concept and is perfectly warranted without any violation to the original text. Kittel discusses this word in relation to other gifts:

> The reference can only be to the specific gifts which qualify a Christian to be a helmsman to his congregation, i.e., a true director of its order and therewith of its life. What was the scope of this directive activity in the time of Paul we do not know. This was a period of fluid development. The importance of the helmsman increases in a time of storm. The office of directing the congregation may well have developed especially in emergencies both within and without. The proclamation of the Word was not originally one of its tasks. The apostles, prophets and teachers saw to this . . . No society can exist without some order and direction. It is the grace of God to give gifts which equip for government. The striking point is that when in verse 29 Paul asks whether all are apostles, whether all are prophets or whether all have gifts of healing, there are no corresponding questions in respect of *antilenpseis and kubernesis.* There is a natural reason for this. If necessary, any member of the congregation may step in to serve as deacon or ruler. Hence these offices, as distinct from those mentioned in verse 29, may be elective. But this does not alter the fact that for their proper discharge the *charisma* of God is indispensable.[2]

The word *kubernēsis* is also found in the Old Testament, mainly in the Wisdom Literature. Three references in Proverbs will suffice. The first is in Proverbs 1:5: "That the wise man may hear, and increase in learning; and that the man of understanding may attain unto sound counsels" (ASV). Here the writer states that a leader or administrator who has the right understanding will direct others in the right course. In Proverbs 11:14, the writer prophesies that where no administration exists, the people will flounder. "Where no wise guidance is, the people falleth; but in the multitude of counsellors there is safety" (ASV). And in Proverbs 24:6, the writer uses the term in a military way. Only the wise strategists or administrators will win a battle. "For by wise guidance thou shalt make thy war; and in the multitude of counsellors there is safety" (ASV).

The practical emphasis of these Greek words which denote leadership responsibility is important for us to consider. It would follow, first, that the gift of administration carries with it executive ability or skill which comes by developing the gift of leadership. Any Christian leader who is placed in a management role and does not try to develop the capacity for administrative oversight would be just as foolish as the minister who has the gift for preaching but does not open a book in sermon preparation.

Second, in the early church it was essential for the evangelists and pastors to appoint people to carry on the work in local congregations. For example, deacons were appointed to administer the charity of the Jerusalem church. If pastors today do not have the gift of administration, they should find others to ease the burden, those who perhaps have better judgment in matters of management.

Third, a Christian leader's style will be determined by what he considers administration. If he sees it as a necessary evil, he will not put his heart and soul into it. Then the organization will suffer, and administration will appear to him as unspiritual and nonessential. If he believes it is essential, his organization will have dynamic growth.

Fourth, for a helmsman to be able to do his job aboard a ship, he must have the full cooperation of the whole crew. Is there not a vital lesson to be learned here? An administrator must be able to work with people and get along with them. He can best do this by helping to develop the skills of his associates and subordinates and then taking a continuing, strong, personal interest in their affairs. This is biblical administration at its best.

In the early church, as the burning zeal of the apostolic church resulted in many converts, the expansion was too great to place all the administrative duties in the hands of one or two people. There were so many demands on the apostles that it became necessary to create a lower echelon of leaders to care for the people. Thus men were carefully chosen to help. "Wherefore, brethren, look ye out among you seven men of honest report, full of the Holy Ghost and wisdom, whom we may appoint over this business" (Acts 6:3).

God directed the apostles to select men with unique gifts to encounter the problems. Dissension arose in the first church at Jerusalem over the matter of dispensing charity. Jewish background is helpful to understand the situation. No nation existed with more social awareness and sense of responsibility for needy people than the Jews. In the synagogue it was a routine custom to care for the needy. There were two kinds of collections to meet this need: there was a fund called the *kuppah,* meaning basket, where individuals collected gifts in the market places; another custom was called the *tamhui,* meaning tray, where collections were made from house to house.

At the time of the writing of the Book of Acts essentially two kinds of Jews were living in Palestine. There were the native people who spoke Aramaic, and the foreign Jews, who had forgotten Hebrew — they spoke Greek or their native tongue. Many had come for the pilgrim feast of Pentecost and remained in Jerusalem for a while. Ill-feeling seemed to develop among the two groups, and this contempt found its way into the daily distribution of alms.

The controversy spilled over into the church because it comprised primarily Jews. A complaint arose that the widows of the Greek-speaking Jews were being deliberately neglected. The apostles felt they could not get mixed up in the matter, so they appointed seven men to straighten out the issue. These were laymen whose very first concern was to put Christianity into practical action. The apostles, therefore, under the guidance of the Holy Spirit, corrected the problem by administering the whole program in a well-devised plan. These early deacons carried out the strategy, and the dissension subsided.

SPECIAL FUNCTIONS

That God calls people for specific functions and ministries to enhance the growth of the church is very evident. Several additional passages warrant our consideration.

Ephesians 4:11-16 discloses one of the apostle Paul's lists of those special functions. Here we see that for the church to be keyed to its prime task of presenting Christ to the world, certain people are singled out, given special qualities of leadership.

It appeared that the apostles and prophets ranked first among the leaders of the early church. As noted, they were to administer the expansion of the church. The apostles were those who had been with Jesus in His earthly ministry or had been witnesses to His resurrection. Of course, when they died out, none could take their place because of their unique credentials. So others were selected because of the evidences of leadership gifts; they were ordained to provide the necessary authentication and witness to the actual existence of Christ and His work to redeem sinful humanity.

The prophets had gifts to give guidance to the Christian communities and to declare God's will. For example, in Acts 13:1-4 they spoke about the first missionary journey. The evangelists preached the good news about the risen Christ. These two functions were for the purpose of preaching and proclaiming the salvation offered by Christ.

The pastor-teachers (Eph. 4) were the shepherds who were more closely related to administration. They were probably the equivalent of "the bishops" (Phil. 1:1) and "the elders" (Acts 20:17). In our earlier discussion we saw that the local Jewish communities had elders who looked after its affairs. These men formed a court to administer justice and also to arrange the worship in the Jewish synagogues. From the earliest of times in Israel's history the elders were looked up to as distinct leaders in the community.

Because the early church was primarily Jewish, it was most natural that it followed the structure and polity of the synagogue. Therefore elders were chosen to lead the people. We are told in Acts 14:23 that Paul and Barnabas appointed elders for each congregation they founded. Besides giving guidance to the church, they gave instruction to the believers on how best to live the Christian life.

The work of those with such an administrative gift is capsulized in Ephesians 4:12. Through the efforts of the leaders, the believers were to be perfected, or completed for growth, so they could capably carry on the work of the ministry. Leaders were called upon to "equip the saints for the work of the ministry"!

Those who displayed unique leadership ability were singled out. In 2 Timothy, Paul reminded his young friend of the time when he was actually ordained to the ministry through the laying on of hands. There is reference to this also in 1 Timothy 4:14. The early church practiced this custom as a form of recognition of a person who had special gifts to lead.

This rite of consecration was inherited from the Jewish practice of consecrating elders in the synagogue. In Judaism the rite meant ordination of a man to the rabbinate.

The practice of laying on hands was initiated during the wilderness wanderings of the Israelites (Deut. 34:9). This reference records the time when Moses turned the nation's leadership over to Joshua; through the laying on of hands, Moses recognized that Joshua had the same spirit and leadership gifts he himself possessed and that Joshua was qualified to be his successor. The initial command for Moses to do this is found in Numbers 27:18.

In the New Testament, the practice was for the purpose of ordaining men to the ministry, as in Timothy's case. The church also ordained for specific tasks, such as when Barnabas and Saul set out for their first missionary journey (Acts 13:2,3). In both cases the act symbolized the church's approval and recognition that the one being ordained was uniquely called and appointed by God for leadership.

Paul's purpose in reminding Timothy of his belief and commitment was to inspire him to further growth. It is always a great boost for a young believer to receive encouragement from others, particularly from those who are older or who hold positions of leadership. The appeal to one's ambitions and potential creates a positive desire for more effective use of the gifts one possesses for leadership.

Timothy was challenged to stir up this gift of leadership which had been confirmed when he was ordained (2 Tim. 1:6). He was reminded of the qualities which should characterize a Christian leader. Each of us can think of a person — or persons — whom God has used to model leadership to us, whose unspoken influence has meant much. There flashes through my mind a half-dozen men who have influenced my life and leadership beyond description.

In conclusion, it is well for us to bear in mind the importance of singling out those who display administrative and leadership qualities — whether they be practicing those gifts in or out of the institutional church — and to do all we can to enhance and encourage their development. Thus the lives of many will be blessed and fulfilled, Christians will be more useful than ever, and their influence in this growing evil world will be more effective.

Notes

[1]Gerhard Kittel, *Theological Dictionary of the New Testament*, vol. III (Grand Rapids: Wm. B. Eerdmans, 1965), s.v. "Kubernesis," pp. 1035 ff.
[2]Ibid.

CHAPTER SIX
Boundaries of Leadership

It is futile to copy another man — the ideal blend is to use your own natural gifts and then develop other leadership traits through diligent work.

In the last chapter we saw how church history reveals that at certain points in time the Holy Spirit spoke directly to people at crisis moments. In the hour of full surrender He released gifts and qualities that often remain latent for a time. This raises some legitimate questions: If God provides the gifts, are there some people then who are born leaders? What about natural abilities? If a person has the gift of leadership, does this preclude special training?

Qualities of leadership cannot be solely explained on the ground of natural ability when we review the lives of such men as Martin Luther, John Hus, Bernard of Clairvaux, and John Wesley. Martin Luther, for example, was out for a walk one day, when a bolt of lightning almost killed him. In a dazed stupor he cried out in terror: "St. Ann, save me, and I'll go to a monastery!" This was not his conversion, but God used such an experience to motivate him for later service in a remarkable way.

Were these people born leaders because God touched their lives in a remarkable way? We think not. It appears that in the secular world, in both the political arena and the hard-driving, complex business and industrial world, men get to the top because they manifest a strong ego and forceful personality. This drive may cause us to believe that they are natural leaders.

What About "Born Leaders"?

Historically this kind of leader is usually thought of as being a "born leader." Yet he leads only because circumstances make it so. He came on the scene at just the time when a particular situation demanded leadership. It can be said that he does not function apart from the demands of a confluence of circumstances outside of himself.

In this mold we often place the Napoleons, the Hitlers, and the Stalins — the conquerors, dictators, and despots — the dominant egotists who have shown characteristics of leadership. Usually this kind has pushed himself into power through might, military aggression, and seizure of political power.

But this kind of leader is often very weak, for he can only impose his authority over others through a neurotic will to power that is inordinate and insatiable. There are undoubtedly times and places where such personalities provide unity of purpose and clarity of intention for which people yearn. But in time they fade in popularity and accomplishment.

Adolf Hitler probably would never have accomplished his goals if the German people had not been "ready" due to the political and economic insecurity in the 1920s and early 1930s. Many were persuaded that Nazism was a good cause to be served for the sake of Germany. Unfortunately, as they found out later when they couldn't change the situation, they realized they followed not a leader, but a tyrant.

This kind of leader is found not only in the political world, but in most other spheres of life. They are the paternalistic, autocratic managers who keep control by arbitrarily deciding what is good for people. Often they are well-intentioned and come through as the kind of person who always wants to give others a fair deal. They appear to be accessible at all times. We do not want to disparage the individualistic kind of leader, but it is important to recognize his limitations, because he does not produce independent, creative thinking, nor does he help in providing for changes for the better within a group structure.

Another problem for the autocratic leader is that the support of his followers is not permanent. Sacrificial loyalty lasts only for a time. A rule of one ministers only to the ego of the ruler. He cannot be a solid and effective leader, because he does not consider the desires and aspirations of his followers.

I knew a young man who decided he wanted to be a strong, natural leader. He decided this would take the form of preaching, so he went to seminary. A friend knew of his high ambition. One day the two were talking about the qualities needed in a leader. The friend said, "Let me look at your library."

After browsing through it, he returned and said, "Look, all you've got is Greek, Hebrew, apologetics, and philosophy. Where are your biographies?"

The reply was "What do I need them for? I'm going to preach."

The friend answered, "You need to read biographies to be a leader."

So the young man went out and purchased a number of biographies, written about strong, natural leaders.

After reading a number of them, he found them to be a hindrance. He had read about Wesley, Taylor, Studd, Whitefield, Edwards, Spurgeon. He wanted to pattern his life and ministry after them, but concluded he was more than ever in bondage and all the more frustrated. He prayed — all night — that God would make him a natural leader. Then one morning sometime later he awakened to discover that God really wanted him just as He had made him.

You see, a person has to accept himself just as he is — not in a moral sense, but in the sense of personality and competence in the gifts God has granted. We have no more and no less. We can develop the gifts He has given us, but it is futile to imitate another person: it invariably brings disillusionment, despair, and discouragement.

CAN WE TRAIN LEADERS?

The genuine Christian leader must always have the humility not to feel threatened by those close to him. Often congregations suffer because there are men on the ministerial staff who find it difficult to function in a staff relationship. Rivalries build, and deprecation of others sets in. This means effective training is required. The true Christian leader will always want to be trained, teaching and encouraging others to assist and to follow. This does not mean that he will relinquish position or control, or be threatened in his leadership role.

Can individuals be trained for leadership? As previously stated, it was assumed for centuries that leadership was inherited or passed on from generation to generation. Leaders were born — not made.

When the feudal system was overthrown by a new burst of freedom in Europe due to the Renaissance, a new concept of leadership took place. Leaders could now be trained and developed, and the focus was shifted to a person's personality and skills which might be latent, waiting for development.

Church and missionary organizations today are faced with the same issue, due to the great need of developing the indigenous church in the Third World where younger churches are ministering. Much training is required to bring a strong national church into existence and keep it healthy.

Christians, because of these needs alone, must believe in the necessity of training leaders.

Consider that a number of people in the Bible were trained for places of leadership even though they had received a call from God. The best example is probably the disciples, who were trained at the feet of Jesus for three years. In His high priestly prayer to the Father before His death, Jesus alluded to those things which He had passed on to the Twelve in order to perpetuate His work on earth. ''For I have passed on to them the commands you gave me; and they took them and know of a certainty that I came down to earth from you, and they believe you sent me'' (John 17:8 LB).

TRAINING CENTERS

A prophet of God in the Old Testament period was specifically called to enunciate His truths to the world. Yet under Samuel's direction an actual school (the ''School of the Prophets'') was set up to train the prophets (1 Sam. 19:18-20). It was here that David no doubt found refuge from Saul who at that time wanted to destroy him. During the time of Elijah and Elisha such training schools were located at Gilgal and Bethel and elsewhere (2 Kings 2:1; 4:38; 6:1). According to Jewish tradition, these schools trained students throughout the long history of Judah to fill the office of prophet. There were many of these seers or scribes, for the Old Testament frequently alludes to prophets in the plural.

Such schools were the forerunner of the Jewish rabbinic centers following the return of the captives from Babylon under the direction of Ezra, Nehemiah, and Zerubbabel. The theological schools of the early church were a direct outgrowth of this concept, and the modern seminary is the extension in our time.

The purpose of the schools was always threefold: to develop, train, and educate men in the leadership functions necessary to perpetuate God's work. We may safely conclude that spiritual gifts can be developed.

Other biblical references demonstrate the need and justification for developing gifts within people to place them in positions of leadership. Moses trained his successor Joshua. Joshua was discovered in the battle against the Amalekites; Moses saw his potential immediately and groomed him to become the undisputed leader of the people. In Numbers 27:18 it states that God would give His people direction through the appointment of a man. But the calling required training and supervision. For many years Moses shared his leadership responsibilities with Joshua.

Training was an important part of the formation of the early church and the work of the apostle Paul. Remember that the training of people was the key for the rapid expansion of the church in the first century. Paul trained Timothy, Barnabas, Silas, and John Mark. He was also responsible for the growth of Sopater, Aristarchus, Secundus, Gaius, Tychicus, Trophimus, and others whom he mentions in his epistles.

Paul could have appealed simply to his special gift of apostleship and let it go at that, trying to do all the work himself. But he wisely followed the course of preparing others and helping to establish those with whom he shared the gospel.

Our missionary and evangelical enterprises are doomed today in the Third World if our leaders, both from the West and in the developing nations, do not develop leadership among Christian nationals. Thank God, this seems to be an increasing emphasis in these younger churches in the Third World. People like John Haggai and my World Vision Indian colleague, Dr. Sam Kamaleson, are making a tremendous impact in this ministry.

AN APPROACH TO TRAINING

Richard Wolfe, in *Man at the Top,* sets forth a basic approach for an effective leadership training program for Christians. He suggests that three decisive steps are necessary: (1) a conscious plan to develop leaders; (2) an inventory of leadership positions; and (3) an inventory of potential leaders.

Wolfe says, first, that every organization must continually give much thought to the training of others for positions of authority. Otherwise the organization will grow stagnant. Training provides for constant innovation and a dynamic infusion into the organization, a spirit of success and the direction that employees need. This helps to destroy negativism and encourages personal initiative.

Second, Wolfe suggests a regular "audit" of any organization to place the best people in various areas of responsibility. This requires a strategy with an organization or flow chart. Then an organization can better know its function, find the right people, and train them to meet specific needs. A continuing question is this: should a man make the job, or should the position determine the kind of a man needed? It is generally best to set the parameters of a job and then find or train the most able man to fill the need. An important task of management and leadership is to prepare job descriptions so that all participants understand their respective roles and duties.

Third, there should be an ongoing search for potential leaders in any organization. This is done by personal contacts and interviews. Aptitudes, skills, personality, intelligence, motivation, values, judgment, and character are some major considerations in looking for leaders.

In the interview, Wolfe says, the dialogue should cover the following:

> Sensitivity, the ability to see something to which the average person is blind;
> The capacity to stretch perceptual powers;
> Flexibility, the ability to adjust quickly to new developments;
> Openness, a willingness to abandon old ways and to move beyond the obvious boundaries of the problem;
> The courage to establish norms;
> The ability to abstract, breaking down problems into component parts and combining various elements to form a new whole.[1]

SPIRITUAL LEADERSHIP REQUIRES MORE

Leadership is often mistakenly considered a product of one's natural abilities and personality traits, including his mental capacity, enthusiasm, and power to persuade. These forces at work can go a long way in leading people, but they have limitations. These are not the only, or even the main, ingredients for spiritual leadership.

The main quality is that possessed by Jesus which we discussed earlier: the willingness to sacrifice for the sake of the determined objectives. It is best expressed in a person who is willing to serve others. Election, appointment, or simply holding a person important does not make him a leader. He can possess many fine qualities but still fail as a leader.

Spiritual leadership serves others. God is constantly searching for men with this characteristic (cf. 2 Chron. 16:9). Not all who aspire to spiritual leadership are willing to pay the price of service, and an urgent need today is for more Christians to become public servants who will be more concerned about their community's interests than their own. We can thank God for political leaders such as Senator Mark O. Hatfield and Congressman John B. Anderson who serve God and the public meaningfully.

THE IDEAL BLEND

A leader who is a Christian blends both natural and spiritual qualities. Even his natural gifts are not self-induced, but granted by God. Therefore the Christian leader influences others not only by the power of his own personality, but by a personality empowered by the Holy Spirit.

Put another way, there is no such thing as a self-made spiritual leader. Because spiritual leadership is a matter of superior qualities, it can never be self-generated.

J. Oswald Sanders, formerly director of the Overseas Missionary Fellowship, in his classic book *Spiritual Leadership* respects the view that natural and spiritual leadership may have many points of similarity, but there are important dissimilarities.

Natural	Spiritual
Self-confident	Confident in God
Knows men	Also knows God
Makes own decisions	Seeks to know God's will
Ambitious	Self-effacing
Originates own methods	Finds and follows God's methods
Enjoys commanding others	Delights to obey God
Motivated by personal considerations	Motivated by love for God and man
Independent	God-dependent

Sanders adds, "While conversion does not normally make leaders of people who would never become such otherwise, church history teaches that in the hour of full surrender the Holy Spirit sometimes releases gifts and qualities that have long remained latent and dormant. It is the prerogative of the Spirit to bestow spiritual gifts which greatly enhance the leadership potential of the recipient."[2]

Note that spiritual ends can be achieved only by spiritual men who use Spirit-directed means. That is why unregenerate people, no matter how marvelously gifted they may be with natural talents, cannot function effectively in leadership in Christian enterprises.

WHAT VERSUS WHERE

In considering the boundaries of leadership in a Christian, we must recognize the dynamic tension between a *call* and a *gift*. The Bible clearly states that men are sovereignly given gifts to take up places of leadership in the Christian community. Some leaders receive multiple gifts, it seems, to fulfill functions in churches, literature, communications, education, and world missions.

One contemporary writer makes the distinction between the two in this way: A call is like "the rudder that steers the ship. None of the spiritual gifts delineated in the New Testament has any geographical connotation. No one, for example, has the gift of 'missionary work in Africa' or 'ministry to inner city youth.' The gifts rather describe the *what* of ministry, and the call then designates the *where* of ministry. That is why we should not be upset when a missionary who has been ministering, let us say, in Germany may decide at one point that it is within the will of God for him to switch to a ministry among German-speaking people in Argentina."[3]

Not all who aspire to lead are able, because of prescribed limitations. Some of the apparent boundaries to leadership appear to be a person's spiritual gifts, his technical skills, the situation being faced, one's experience, and the length of the person's experience.

Notes

[1]Richard Wolfe, *Man at the Top* (Wheaton, Ill.: Tyndale House Publishers, 1969), p. 125.
[2]J. Oswald Sanders, *Spiritual Leadership* (Chicago: Moody Press, 1967), pp. 21-22.
[3]Kenneth O. Gangel, *Competent to Lead* (Chicago: Moody Press, 1974), p. 40.

CHAPTER SEVEN
Styles of Leadership

The appropriate style depends a great deal upon the task and phase of the organization as well as the need of the moment.

Management theorists, despairing over their inability to define leadership adequately, frequently attempt to picture it in terms of style. In doing so they describe how the leader operates, rather than what he is. If you give some thought to it you can probably come up with your ideas about style: "He's a player/coach type" or "She's a prima donna" or "He's a one-man show." So we tend to characterize the way a leader leads by our own perceptions.

The emphasis on human skills was considered important in the past, but it is of primary importance today. The great American entrepreneur John D. Rockefeller stated, "I will pay more for the ability to deal with people than any other ability under the sun." According to a report by the American Management Association, an overwhelming majority of the two hundred managers who participated in a survey agreed that the most important single skill of an executive is his ability to get along with people. In the survey, management rated this ability more vital than intelligence, decisiveness, knowledge, or job skills.

Style, by definition, is the way a leader carries out his functions and how he is perceived by those he attempts to lead.

The more a leader adapts his style of leadership behavior to meet the particular situation and the needs of his followers, the more effective he becomes in reaching personal and organizational goals.

The concept of leadership behavior questions the existence of a "best" style of leadership: it is a matter, not of the best style, but of the most effective style for a particular situation. A number of leader-behavior styles may be effective or ineffective depending on the important elements of the situation, as we note in this chapter.

Empirical studies tend to show that there is no normative (best) style of leadership. Successful leaders adapt their leader behavior to meet the needs of the group and the particular situation.

Leadership can be exercised in numerous ways, whether it is exerted in academic, political, military, artistic, religious, economic, or social spheres.

You undoubtedly have heard the question asked, "Have events throughout history made great men, or is it that great men have made events happen?" The answer probably lies in a combination of both, but the style or quality of leadership at a given point in time has produced either positive or negative effects.

From student body president to president of the United States, from preschool teacher to college professor, leadership relates to every aspect of human endeavor. Everyone is interested in style as much as the person's philosophy or purpose in leadership. So the issue is more than academic — it is intensely practical.

THE EXISTING CONDITION

The style of leadership depends upon several factors: the personality, the character or needs of the group to be supervised, and the immediate situation (which the German rationalists called the *Sitz in Leben* – "the seat in life," or life setting).

Whether we talk of government, business, or the church, moods or conditions at the time often dictate the kind of leader who emerges to meet the situational demands. Church history abounds with illustrations of people who became leaders because of an existing condition. Whenever the church found itself at a low ebb spiritually or morally, God raised up men like Athanasius, Tertullian, Augustine, Bernard of Clarivaux, Anselm, Luther, Calvin, Knox, Wesley. In our day the success of Billy Graham is due at least in part to the pressures of modern life, the secularization of the church, and the impersonal philosophy of collectivism. Man is viewed as a machine to be controlled or manipulated. True to the authority of Scripture, Graham's message emphasizes God's continuing interest in the individual, thereby bringing meaning and purpose to the hungry and longing soul who searches for meaning and an adequate philosophy of life. The times determined his style.

The Bible is a graphic illustration also of styles, displaying the emergence of men who were uniquely fitted for the task of leadership. The effective leader must always consider the present existential consideration. This does not mean that a person must capitalize or be an opportunist to gain advantage over his confreres, but it does mean he must be alert to the needs people have, to their attitudes in face of crisis and decision, and to the best methodology for getting the best results for the most people possible. He must know the crucial point, the decisive moment for action. Solomon illustrated this point when he built the temple: he seized upon the opportunity and the need of the moment to unify the Israelites with a national purpose.

The existing condition usually cannot be manufactured — it does not emerge from a vacuum. A leader cannot create a condition; he has to keep in step with the times and make the best of the situation.

The Christian leader must also recognize his personality and gifts, the needs of the people, and the given condition. He cannot be driven by the thirst for power.

A leader who discerns the times is able to clarify and suggest the best course of action. He has flexibility, for should the existing conditions change, he is able to adjust and be equally effective. Many organizations lose ground or become less effective because their leadership is not imaginative or creative enough to keep up with the times. "We've always done it this way in the past, why change?" is the prevailing mood. Maintaining the status quo is lethal.

Not only must the situation dictate the best style, but also the challenge of the task. This means the leader must be in tune with himself — his character and personality structure and his motivational level. He has to know the style most comfortable for himself, and he must analyze the group for whom he is responsible. Are the individuals within the group capable of responsibility and decision making? Do they know the goals, and what is their past performance? Have we prepared them to accept delegated responsibility and authority?

It is important to distinguish between management and leadership. In essence, leadership is a broader concept than management. Management is thought of as a special kind of leadership in which the accomplishment of organizational goals is paramount. While leadership also involves working with and through people to accomplish goals, these are not necessarily organizational goals.

STYLE IS CRITICAL

Not long ago a report was submitted by the Northwest Friends churches which presented a study made of growth patterns of churches.[1] Sixty churches were studied, showing statistics for attendance, age, and average income of each. Also, questions were asked to disclose the attitudes and thinking of the various leaders.

Unsurprisingly the findings showed that different styles determined whether a church was static or growing. The leaders in the dynamic situations were characterized as positive, confident, cheerful, and goal-oriented. They always tried to involve as many people in the congregation as possible.

The static churches, on the other hand, had leaders with little vision and little creative imagination. Goal-setting, the report said, is unquestionably the most important ingredient needed for growth. Leaders who are not visionary enough stifle church growth. Usually they are inflexible as well, without the ability to delegate work because they do not trust others.

This study can be a model for churches everywhere. Style is critical.

WHAT LEADERSHIP STYLES ARE THERE?

Because leadership style includes how a person functions or operates within the context of his group or organization, it is perhaps easiest to discuss the subject by describing the kind of situation that either results from or is appropriate to a particular style. My focus now is on those who are already in positions of leadership, rather than those aspiring to it. It is, therefore, vital for them to examine their own methods of managing and/or leading people.

There may be as many different leadership styles as there are types of people, but they fall into several main categories. The styles could also be thought of as methods of management. Much has been written on this subject. Contributions range from the "autocrat-bureaucrat-democrat" grouping to the "managerial grid" based on a vertical coordinate of concern for people and a horizontal coordinate of concern for production.

Several modern views reject the idea that firm and tightly structured styles of leadership are effective. Rather, there are combinations of styles leaders use as required by the demands of the position, the composition of the personnel being led, the individual leader's personality, and the expectation of the company.

In *Managing Your Time* I briefly discuss five basic categories from which all the other combinations emanate: "(1) *laissez-faire*: No structure or supervision given; members set own goals and standards of performance; leader is 'first among equals,' without authority, a resource man; (2) *democratic-participative*: provides some structure and framework within which members still largely set own goals and standards; leader and advisor with minimum authority; (3) *manipulative-inspirational*: some structure, usually confused and ambiguous; goals set by management with little participation but employees' acceptance sought by 'hard sell'; (4) *benevolent-autocratic*: activities of group largely structured; relatively close supervision; however, employees encouraged to make suggestions concerning their goals, working conditions, etc.; (5) *autocratic-bureaucratic*: activities of group totally and arbitrarily structured; participation by group in any context totally discouraged; supervision is authoritarian and autocratic; questioning of orders regarded as insubordinate.''[2]

Using this list as a guide, let us describe various types in more detail and look at them in terms of how the leader operates within the organization.

LAISSEZ-FAIRE

This kind of a leader gives minimum direction and provides maximum freedom for group decisions. He recedes into the background, allowing others to express themselves. He establishes rapport and remains silent until his specific direction or opinion is called for. His role is similar to the nondirective approach in psychological therapy. This view operates on the assumption that man himself and society contain remedial forces to allow a strong, healthy relationship between the leader and the group. This permits growth through group decision.

Actually we could say that this style is practically no leadership at all and allows everything to run its own course. The leader simply performs a maintenance function. For example, a pastor may act as a figurehead and concern himself only with his pulpit ministry while others are left to work out the details of how the church is to function.

This style lends itself best to those leaders who are away a lot or who have been temporarily put in charge.

DEMOCRATIC-PARTICIPATIVE

The democratic concept is a relatively new idea in world history. Previously control was in the hands of one person or a distinct elite. But democracy describes a form of government or leadership where decisions are made for the people through representation. It follows that a leader carries out the needs of the group and helps to define more sharply their aspirations.

The emphasis is upon the group through participation of the collective. Policies become the group decision. The leader in this kind of structure is there to assist, suggest, and allow adequate communication to flow so the entire group is alerted to problems and so the people can resolve them.

This style is used by those who believe the way to motivate others is to involve them in decision making. This hopefully creates goal ownership and a feeling of shared purpose.

Studies involving thousands of supervisors at all levels have proved that leadership style in any organization is a major determinant of employee productivity. For example, the best records of performance are found where the primary attention of the leader is on the human aspect of their subordinates' problems, allowing them to help make decisions.

Certainly one way to accomplish a high level of production is by letting people do the job the way they want to as long as they accomplish the objective. This may mean letting them take time out from the monotony. They should also be made to feel they are something special and not just run-of-the-mill. If employees are kept from feeling put upon, they are far more apt to expend the needed effort to get the work completed on time.

By contrast, the less successful leader is one who probably has an interest in people but considers it a type of luxury. The attitude is "I've just got to keep the pressure on for production sake, and when I get production up, then I can afford to take more time to show an interest in my people."

Studies made at many large corporations conclude that motivation is strongly related to the supervisory style of the immediate boss. This would be equally true in Christian organizations. People are people no matter where you find them. Strong supervisors stimulate motivation; weak supervisors inhibit it. Interviews with all kinds of people show that practically everyone prefers a developmental, people-oriented supervisor regardless of their own values or the style they themselves practice.

Sometime ago an excellent article set forth the necessary qualities needed in groups if they were to be led by a free, democratic leader or administration:

If the subordinates have relatively high needs for independence.

If the subordinates have a readiness to assume responsibility for decision-making.

If they have a relatively high tolerance for ambiguity.

If they are interested in the problem and feel that it is important.

If they have the necessary knowledge and experience to deal with the problem.

If they have learned to expect to share in decision-making.[3]

It must be recognized that every style has its own problems or limitations. The democratic approach cannot answer every situation. For example, when an impasse is reached and a stalemate lingers, possibly the only way out is to appoint a committee or give a responsible person the power to act and make a decision. This can often create the illusion that action was taken, regardless of what the result may be, due to slow progress or the group's lacking adequate communication or education.

Another weakness of this style is that it can sink to the level of mediocrity because it is so easy to "pass the buck" and shirk responsibility. It is easy to fall prey to the attitude that "he'd rather be popular than be right." This style or emphasis can be effective only when there is a balance between allowing group participation on the one hand and being able to make solo decisions when they are necessary to save time.

Perhaps the greatest weakness of the democratic style is that in times of crisis there is usually much costly delay in action.

BENEVOLENT-AUTOCRATIC

This style is characterized by the fatherlike concern the leader has for his people. We could also call this method the "paternalistic" style. The autocratic leaders cannot get too close, but the paternal leader identifies closely with the group.

Here the desire is to keep everyone in the group satisfied and happy. It is assumed that if people feel good because of a paternal leader, the organization will function well.

Identification, however, tends to make the people in the group too dependent and weak. It can degenerate into mere admiration and pseudoworship. Also, when this kind of leader is removed from the scene, the organization flounders.

This "family" approach appeals because it creates the illusion of security and fellowship, but this is at the expense of efficiency and effectiveness. Discipline is hard to maintain, and coordination often suffers with this style.

AUTOCRATIC-BUREAUCRATIC

The extreme of the democratic style is the "one rule" type of leadership. This is often found in Christian groups and organizations, because people tend to regard some as being led in this direction by the will of God. Many of our "Christian entrepreneur" types fall into this mode, and in recent years we have witnessed strong and effective ministries irreparably harmed because this kind of leader failed to recognize this as a leadership weakness and thus not delegate responsibilities or have colleagues share in them.

In business this style is marked by a continual reference to organization rules and regulations, because it leans toward the authority of a person or system. The style assumes that people will not do anything unless told to, and the leader sees himself as being indispensable because he is "the only one who really knows what's going on" and he alone can make decisions quickly.

The bureaucratic leader assumes that somehow difficulties can be ironed out if everyone will abide by the rules. As a diplomat he learns how to use the majority rule as a way to get people to perform.

I suppose the concentration of power in one man in historical examples grew out of the critical emergency of military campaigns. When victory was obtained, people were dazzled by the splendor of the achievement, and this easily led to despotism and totalitarianism.

The autocratic style can sometimes be misleading, especially when people are made to believe they have some say in the planning and future of an organization or government. This is illustrated best by the modern Marxist-Leninist movement, which falsely maintains the view that "power belongs to the people." Many of the Communist states are known as "People's Republics." After World War II, Germany was divided; East Germany became known as the German Democratic Republic. One West German official remarked that the new nation was not German, nor was it democratic nor a republic, but a Soviet colony, ruled by the despots in Moscow. Millions of people in our day know the lie of Communist propaganda and the terror of autocratic rule. Mao Tse-tung more aptly describes such rule in his "Little Red Book": "Power only comes out of the barrel of a gun."

The leader using this style, whether in government, industry, or a Christian organization, answers to no one. He seldom hesitates, and he moves ahead independent of human feeling. He uses people and rides their aspirations to increase his authority. He often gets their consent for decisions, but this is done by manipulation, hiding the true facts, and through the means of control and threat.

There are times, perhaps, where this style provides strength and unity, but on the whole its weaknesses are most glaring.

One of Napoleon's generals allegedly said, "You can do everything with swords except sit on them." The autocratic style is 99 percent inflexible. There is no check and balance system to test weaknesses. The leader may point to the ultimate goal as being positive and beneficial to all. However, if the means to achieve that goal is cruel, harsh, tyrannical, and destructive, then the goal is no greater than the means.

The writer of Proverbs reminds us that people are important and to run roughshod over them is detrimental: "Without people a prince is ruined" (Prov. 14:28 RSV). We have often heard the statement made famous during the last century, "Power tends to corrupt; absolute power corrupts absolutely." It does so because people are made to be slaves and paupers as pawns in the hands of weak leaders who can rule only by force. Malice, intolerance, and suspicion are the fruits of this kind of style because resentment issues from feelings of injustice and corrupted power.

One has only to read the Book of Nehemiah to discover the importance of people at work. The leaders in rebuilding the temple and city walls never lost sight of the total goal and overall picture, and they knew they could not do it all. They were able to keep this in focus by using all the people as well as experts who were trained to do specific jobs (cf. 2 Chron. 2:14 ff.).

The bureaucratic leader is narrow, an extremist. He is often fanatical because he thinks provincially, exclusive of other groups. He is often ethnically bigoted. This kind of person has strong convictions, but more often than not cannot accept those in other groups because he has a "party spirit" and sees them as beneath himself or his group.

His intense dedication tends to make this kind of a leader glory in adversity and give him a martyr complex. But his loyalty to just one group cannot enhance the efficiency of the group for very long.

The style of the autocratic-bureaucratic leader is fraught with weaknesses. Historian Arnold Toynbee stated that the rise and fall of societies has a one-to-one correlation with the type of leadership exerted. He reasons that where leaders control by force, that society ceases to grow.

We tend in our society today, because it is an age of specialization, erroneously to equate an expert with authority. But we must be careful. One may become a leader in his own field and achieve; yet, since we are hero worshipers, there is an inherent danger. Frequently a person who has a Ph.D. degree is consulted on matters in fields foreign to his training or expertise; he is often considered an expert in all fields! The truth of the matter is, the higher a person goes in education, often the greater his limitations become. The "expert" does not qualify in unrelated fields any more than another person. In these alien fields he may tend to view all things from his own often limited perspective and can be as mistaken as anyone else regardless of his educational level.

Some writers on leadership have felt that concern for task, work, or ministry tends to be represented by authoritarian leader behavior, while a concern for relationships is represented by democratic leader behavior. This thinking has been popular because it is generally agreed that a leader influences his followers by either of two ways: (1) he can tell his followers what to do and how to do it, or (2) he can share his leadership responsibilities with his followers by involving them in the planning and execution of the task. The former is the traditional authoritarian style that emphasizes task concerns; the latter is the less directive, democratic style that stresses concern for human relationships.

The differences in the two styles are based on the assumptions the leader makes about the source of his authority and about human nature. The authoritarian style often assumes that the leader's power is derived from the position he occupies and that man is innately lazy and unreliable (Theory X); the democratic style assumes that the leader's power is granted by the group he is to lead and that men can be basically self-directed and creative at work if properly motivated (Theory Y). (The concept of theory X and theory Y was first proposed by Douglas MacGregor in his book *The Human Side of Enterprise* [New York: McGraw-Hill, 1960].) Consequently, in the authoritarian style, practically all policies are determined by the leader, while in the democratic style, policies are open for group discussion and decision.

Leaders whose behavior is observed to be relatively authoritarian tend to be task-oriented and use their power to influence their followers. Leaders whose behavior appears to be relatively democratic tend to be group-oriented and thus give their followers considerable freedom in their work. Often this continuum is extended beyond democratic leader behavior to include the laissez-faire style. This style is, as indicated, very permissive. Few policies or procedures are established; everyone is left on his own; none attempts to influence anyone else. A wretched state indeed!

A good leader will be alert constantly for experts who can consult and render advice on specific matters. He will gain the essentials to get the best results. It is good to remember the economic principle of the division of labor; the leader who tries to do it all is doomed to failure.

Another great drawback of this autocratic-bureaucratic style is that it stifles creative action and discourages innovation and any strong inclination toward change. This kind of leader feels threatened by change initiated by others. Thus he usually supports what is conventional. He cannot even support what is middle ground, because for the most part he can accept only extremes like good-bad or black-white. It is hard for him to accept compromise.

This person often has a personality defect. His ego is so weak that he has to identify with the strong or tough. Because he cannot really accept himself, he has little feeling for others. He is like the playground bully who has to raise a front to defend against his weakness, which he dare not disclose.

The authoritarian often is known to have grown up in a home or in circumstances in which he was constantly put down by a rigid authority figure. He was not given the right to express himself or his feelings: he counted for little. Without proper parental guidance in gentleness, kindness, and words of encouragement and compliments for achievement, he never learned to feel good about himself. In adult life he expresses this deprivation to others usually without even knowing it.

Finally, there is a vast difference between leading and commanding. The latter seldom gets results from people working in association. Contrast the two attitudes by the following true illustrations.

A supervisor with a surveying firm once said he never listens to personal problems or complaints from his men. If they don't obey they are simply fired — no questions asked — and a new person is hired. Obviously that firm is not highly successful.

A manager in a large canning company has a vastly different approach. "When we hire people, we are looking for people who want a permanent relationship. We want people who are looking for a career who will be happy with us and we with them. And we spend a lot of money and time building a good foundation for that person, hoping to secure a strong common interest. Especially do we want our foremen to express our company's good will to all so everyone will feel a part of the company." This attitude properly characterizes real leadership.

Persons with a command attitude make untenable assumptions — especially the idea that organizations can be "bossed" into survival. The trouble is that commanders direct organizations, but misdirect people because they do not minister to the whole person. They are oblivious to people, because they tend also to believe that their firm exists solely to fulfill the purpose it is specifically organized to carry out. This is a death warrant, since it does not allow for personal responses even though the overall objective of the firm is acceptable. The attitude that "we're only in business to make money" is very likely to produce many bad decisions, because it is not people-oriented.

In the spiritual realm the parallel would be a church that did nothing but have a Sunday morning worship service. Such a church lacks the insight to see that its chief function beside the worship of

God is helping fellow Christians relate to each other. Most people consider this kind of church too austere to join.

The commander, then, always puts the welfare of his organization above that of the people. The true leader strives to make the two one-and-the-same thing. So commanders direct — and leaders guide and develop individuals so that through the group they may better share in shaping their own destiny.

The true leader organizes effort and gives his people a good feeling about what they are doing. There is no intimidation to get people to work; he knows how to keep morale high. Without him there is little zeal or eagerness on the part of people to do something that may even be important. But enthusiasm and effective mobilization of group efforts are called out and sustained by a good leader. Without him it rarely appears.

World Vision International prints a monthly four-page publication, ''Christian Leadership Letter,'' which my colleague Edward Dayton and I edit. (This letter is available free of charge upon request.) The following material from one of our letters brings the subject of style into sharp focus.

WHICH STYLE IS BEST?

Leaders are different. But so are followers! Which is another way of saying that some situations demand one style of leader, while others demand a different one. Leaders are different. Organizations are different. At any given time the leadership needs of an organization may vary from another time. Since organizations have difficulty continually changing their leaders, it follows that those leaders will need *different styles at different times*. The appropriate style depends a great deal on the *task of the organization,* the *phase of life of the organization,* and the *needs of the moment*.

What are some examples of how the *task of the organization* affects leadership style? A fire department cannot perform without at least some autocratic leadership. When the time comes for the organization to perform, to do what it was designed to do, autocratic leadership is a must. There is no time to sit down and discuss how to attack the fire. One trained person has to decide for the group, and the group must abide by his decision. Later there may be a free discussion on which way will be best next time.

On the other hand, a medical group might best be operated with a permissive style.

An autocratic style may even be needed in a Christian organization. In times of crisis, such as the evacuation of mission personnel or the need to reduce costs radically, the leader often must act unilaterally.

Organizations go through *different phases*. During periods of rapid growth and expansion, autocratic leadership may work very well. For example, the founder of a new Christian organization or the founding pastor of a church is often a figure with charisma who knows intuitively what is to be done and how to do it. Since the vision is his, he is best able to impart it to others without discussion. But during periods of slow growth or consolidation, the organization needs to be much more reflective to become more efficient; participative leadership may be in order. Both considerations need to be tempered by the needs of the moment. Using autocratic leadership may work well for fire fighting (either real or figurative), but it will probably be less than successful in dealing with a personal problem. An emergency in the medical group may demand that someone assume (autocratic) leadership.

Fitting Style to Organization

It follows that ideally a leader should have differing styles. He should be a man for all seasons, shifting from the permissiveness of summer to the demands of winter.

On the other side, the organization needs to adopt *a strategy for effectiveness*, taking into account its needs and its ''product.'' Most voluntary groups and nonprofit organizations are founded on a common vision and shared goals. They have a strategy of *seeking success* (reaching their goals). When the organization is young, the founder can depend on his strength of vision to attract others who share his goals. However, as the organization is successful, other means of maintaining a common vision will be needed.

If the leadership style is not modified to include participative sharing of goals, too often the organization will adopt the strategy of *avoiding failure*. When the organization reaches a size at which an autocratic style will no longer work, the leader who is unable to change to a participative style may be forced (perhaps unknowingly) to adopt a laissez-faire approach. Meanwhile the second level of leadership (now forced to run the organization) is most likely to adopt a bureaucratic style.

Where Are You?

What is your leadership style? A cursory examination of some management literature will help you discover this. Hopefully you will discover that you have exercised different styles of leadership at different times. Do you have evidence that you *can* change your style as needed? Or, as you think of the decisions made in the past six months, do you discover that they were always made the same way (by you, by others, together, or by the bureaucracy)?

WHERE IS YOUR ORGANIZATION?

What kind of leadership does your organization need at this time? What is its task? What phase of organizational growth are you in? What are different needs of this moment? Analyze this with help from your board, leadership team, and members. Are different styles of leadership needed for different aspects of organizational life?

WHERE DO YOU GO FROM HERE?

Review your calendar of meetings for the past two weeks. What happened in those meetings? Did you go to meetings just to announce your own decision (autocratic style)? Did you go to the meeting with a hidden agenda expecting only to get concurrence of the group (autocratic style)? Did you go to the meeting expecting to work with the group to arrive at a decision (participative style)? Did you go expecting to sit back and let others worry about the problem (permissive style)? Or, did you go intending to use the parliamentary procedures to make sure that the ship stayed on an even keel (bureaucratic style)? Perhaps you didn't go at all (laissez-faire)!

If you discovered that you handled each meeting in the same way, you are probably locked into one style and should consider knowingly attempting to modify your style as a function of the situation you are in. By deciding before the meeting the style you will adopt, you will gain the advantage of being able to observe the response of the other members of the meeting.

If you have been limiting yourself to one style, sudden changes will often result in confusion in others. It may be necessary for you to spell out clearly the ground rules as to how you expect the decision-making process to work.

FLEXIBILITY IS THE KEY

Each style has its advantages and weaknesses and must be evaluated against actual life situations, because there are no hard, fast lines drawn between different styles. Frequently a democratic leader will be paternalistic or autocratic, depending upon the situation.

The well-adjusted, mature leader has an advantage because he need not be bound to a single method. He can be flexible without being threatened. Such a wise leader will think carefully about the kind of style best suited for the situation. He will first want to consider his subordinates and how he can best relate to them. Then he can more accurately determine the best style.

In closing, it might be helpful to indicate what I consider the vitally important levels of priority for Christian leadership.

The order is crucial.

First — and obvious — is our commitment to the person of God in Christ. This comes through the personal encounter we have had with the Son of God, the Lord Jesus Christ.

The second commitment, far too often confused with the third, is our commitment to the body of Christ. As the apostle Paul said, "Our body has many parts" and we do belong to each other. The measure of our Christian performance is our love for one another. The apostle John exclaimed, "Behold how they love one another!" This is the hallmark of the Christian. Paul had little to say about evangelism in his epistles, but much to say about our love relationship within the body.

Third is a commitment to the work of Christ or the task that God has given to us. The New Testament calls us to be willing to sacrifice houses, families, and lands to follow Christ. But the *work* of Christ will flow forth from the relationships that exist. Too often I have heard Christian leaders say, "What I do as a leader is so important that I must sacrifice my family." If by this he or she means that the work of Christ is more important than the body of Christ, we must protest that this is not the view of the New Testament. The Bible considers our relationship more important than our accomplishment. God will get His work done! He does not demand that we accomplish great things; He demands that we strive for excellence in our relationships.

In our judgment, effective Christian leadership arises from a proper recognition of these priorities.

Notes

[1]"Friends in the Soaring '70's: A Church Growth Era, Oregon Yearly Meeting of Friends Churches" (Newberg, Ore.: August 1969), p. 121.

[2]Ted Engstrom and R. Alec Mackenzie, *Managing Your Time* (Grand Rapids: Zondervan Publishing House, 1974), pp. 96-97.

[3]Robert Tannenbaum and Warren Schmidt, "Choosing a Leadership Pattern," *Harvard Business Review 36* (March-April 1958):99.

CHAPTER EIGHT

The Personality
of the Leader

The best leaders not only must have faith in God and other people, but must believe in themselves.

To perform many tasks adequately and to lead properly, the leader must be able to inspire the led. As we have stated, it is the leader who determines to a large measure the success or failure of any group or organization. How he views himself goes a long way toward one or the other.

Peter Drucker, a noted authority on management, emphasizes in his books that there is no single "effective personality." He observes that outstanding leaders differ widely in their temperaments and abilities. However, to achieve goals the leader must be able to sustain action. To do this, loyalty must be kept, and it is necessary to communicate the view that in the final analysis the hard and the sacrificial way is the most rewarding and enduring.

A Look Inside

To communicate the need for endurance, the leader has to wrestle with his selfhood. People in a group are quick to detect any lack of assurance, enthusiasm, or conviction communicated by their superiors. If the leader is deficient in these qualities, he will be unable to help his constituency to emerge out of doubt, confusion, or lack of confidence. If he cannot give proper support, there is a real loss in the quality of leadership and the inspiration it should impart.

As enthusiasm is catching, the opposite is also true. Where a leader lacks self-confidence, this tends to be infectious as well. It pervades his every effort.

If a leader has a weak self-concept which affects his convictions, the group will begin to question the benefits of effort and wonder whether any struggle or denial has any measure of worth for any cause.

The leader has to have faith in himself and the goals which have been defined. He must have a philosophy of work and effort that will motivate himself and others. It seems necessary, in short, that the really strong leader should believe in some meaning in human living, in some fruitful outcome of human effort, in some sense that mankind struggles not against, but essentially in harmony with, the animating power of the universe. The best leader has faith in the world as a place where there is a real better and worse, where these are somewhat ascertainable, and where effort toward the good can yield appreciable results.

Only when a leader has such a faith does he possess the essence of the deepest inspiration that people crave to gain from him.

Faith is a vital concept, not only in the realm of personal salvation, but for the good of any operating organization. The Bible defines it in Hebrews 11:1 as "the substance of things hoped for, the evidence of things not seen."

The original language and the background of the passage do not convey the idea that faith is merely a fatuous trust, wishful thinking, or wistful longing.

Faith is not a hope that takes refuge in a person, but a corroboration that such a thing will actually take place. The word *substance* conveys the idea of a title deed in the possession of a person. He is not awaiting ownership of property in heaven, but already has possessed it. This is the biblical emphasis. Such a knowledge dominates the Christian's actions when he fully realizes what is rightfully his through Christ.

In like manner a leader must have faith to get from point A to point B in this life. To accomplish this, he needs, first of all, faith in people. He must be able to trust people and believe that they desire to be led. When he believes this, he will be better qualified to tap the sources of human desire. From this will spring hope, meaning, and growth. Without faith in people, futility and pessimism abound.

The greatest leaders have always had a strong faith in themselves to lead. Most have felt somehow that they were instruments of destiny under God. Billy Graham often speaks of himself as being simply the voice of God, yet what authority he commands as he constantly declares, "The Bible says!"

It is vital for people to develop a larger view of themselves to provide a more satisfying sense of values and reality as they seek to motivate others. When failures occur and seemingly insurmountable obstacles appear, refusing to admit defeat will often win the day. It takes a person with a strong and sanctified ego to overcome limitations. He must rely upon himself, his knowledge, his powers of discernment, and his motivation. But the leader must also derive support from spiritual resources outside himself, because there will be many periods of loneliness. Leadership is lonely! He may be ignored or even betrayed by people he felt he could count on. Spiritual faith is a demand even when the objectives are material or secular in nature.

The fruit of strong faith is a serenity that rises above turmoil and provides balance when the leader must stand against many odds. These are essential for a successful leader. Without them, discouragement and despair can easily set in.

A person with low self-esteem has many difficulties. This is especially so for a leader, because his view of others reflects how he sees himself. If he does not feel good about himself as a human being, he will not be an inner-directed individual, but will constantly have to be bolstered and motivated by people around him.

History clearly shows that the most achieving people in all the world have a basic thing in common — they were inner-directed people. Without inner direction, a person has a problem in decision making. He struggles to be decisive and convincing. Such struggles cannot affect the lives and destinies of other people positively.

You have heard it said that it is better to try something and be a failure than never to try at all. People with a weak self-concept usually are a liability to an organization because they seldom take risks necessary to achieve higher goals.

But the emotionally mature person can cope with possible failure and weakness because it does not devastate him to the point of self-pity. He can use the failure as a learning experience and marshal the drive to try again. The essayist Carlyle put it well: "The block of granite which was an obstacle in the pathway of the weak becomes a stepping stone in the pathway of the strong."

RECOGNIZING YOUR IDENTITY

Uniqueness and individuality are important qualities for a leader. They contribute toward knowing oneself. Individuality is not to be confused with rebellion or isolation or refusing interaction with others; rather, it is the process of interaction. It may also be described as the condition of a human-being-in-a-group that causes a person to be perceived by himself as distinctive within the group.

A leader has to recognize that he can only know himself as he is seen and experienced by others. He cannot be autonomous, but is an inseparable part of the group to which he belongs. Because God has made us social creatures, we are incomplete individuals without group interaction. Call it *fellowship* if you will.

This does not deny a person his freedom or democratic heritage or give any group priority. The leader must feel his uniqueness and be able to proceed from it. Today this is becoming more and more difficult because of the standardization of so many things. The secularistic, collectivized state militates against uniqueness because it accentuates similarities and not the differences. In this day we may be grateful for the strong reemphasis in the Christian world of the doctrine of spiritual gifts. This biblical notion is a fresh wind in an era which would seek to reduce all men to replaceable cogs in the machinery of production.

Under stress, the leader may temporarily confuse his identity. He should, for example, recognize that behavior acceptable at an office party may be inappropriate on the job the next day: he might confuse the hearty friendliness of his superior at the party and attempt to respond the same way on the next day of business. As there is a time and place for everything, there is an individual sensitivity for each time and place. Uniqueness and individuality, when recognized by a leader, permit him much satisfaction and adjustment to respective situations and groups. The leader must know himself and be a mature human being.

A MARK OF MATURITY

To be the most effective kind of leader, one must possess emotional stability. Such stability can be measured only in the way a person copes with anxiety or conflict and the way he relates to or deals with others.

Every human being experiences tension, frustration, and conflicts with other people. If he does not, he is either psychotic or withdrawing from the mainstream of life. A mark of maturity is the ability to handle conflict. This includes the ability to deal with realities as to what can and cannot be changed. A mature executive said to me, "I have learned never to fret over something that I cannot change." Such an approach to life is evidence of stability. The ability to make those necessary compromises with what cannot be changed largely determines whether one will be successful as a social being.

Anxiety is the key to personality development because it provides a test for the ego. There is a proverb: "The stronger the wind, the mightier the oak becomes." The way a person deals with conflict does denote whether he is a strong, healthy, emotional person, or one who develops neurotic symptoms. The way an individual thinks of himself and others greatly determines how he will face tension. If he has a weak ego, he will continually rely on defense structures that sustain neuroticism and prevent emotional growth. This blocks and complicates communication with others and causes interpersonal relations to disintegrate.

A leader must be mindful that his emotional stability is indicated in the way he deals with people. Such characteristics as understanding, trust, confidence, tolerance, loyalty, and sympathy are the ingredients that disclose emotional maturity.

Immaturity also may be characterized in a number of ways. Leaders who evidence immaturity usually fail. It manifests itself in people through their involvement with others in some of the following ways:

1. They have little tact in getting along with people.
2. They interfere in others' affairs.
3. They constantly resist change because of their underlying insecurities.
4. They blame others when things go wrong.
5. They are not able to develop in their organization a solid esprit de corps because it is difficult for them to be a part of a team.
6. They cannot handle criticism and differences in others.
7. They are overly critical of other people and their methods of doing things.
8. They cannot cut through trivia and help a group reach the major goals and objectives.

Maxwell Maltz has written an outstanding work dealing with the self-concept. He says,

> The person who feels that people are not very important cannot have very much deep-down self-respect and self-regard — for he himself is "people" and with what judgment he considers others, he himself is unwittingly judged in his own mind. . . .
>
> One of the best known methods of getting over a feeling of guilt is to stop condemning other people in your own mind — stop judging them — stop blaming them and hating them for their mistakes. You will develop a better and more adequate self-image when you begin to feel that other people are more worthy. Practice treating other people as if they had some value — and surprisingly enough your own self-esteem will go up.[1]

It is true that leaders who lack a good self-concept can do a lot of bluffing, but it will eventually take its toll when frustration sets in.

KNOWING YOUR TRAITS

Leaders need to be creative thinkers and innovators with the ability to extend themselves but not stifle action. To do this they need to develop strong personality traits. A trait may be defined as a person's characteristic act, thought, or feeling that is inherited or acquired. It is a quality or ability that a person possesses. A leadership trait is a distinguishing personal quality that enables a person to exercise certain abilities. A good leader not only will become aware of his self-image, but will know his peculiar strengths and attempt to increase his effective use of them for the good of the group. Among the most important traits needed by a leader are intelligence, dependability, sociableness, loyalty, friendliness, and faithfulness.

A good leader must have the added ability to look beyond himself and perceive the traits in others that are most essential for the good of the organization.

Some traits are common to all who are effective spiritual leaders.

First is *enthusiasm*. This trait includes both optimism and hope. No pessimist ever made a great leader. The pessimist sees a difficulty in every opportunity; the optimist sees an opportunity in every difficulty. "An optimist laughs to forget — and a pessimist forgets to laugh." A leader thinks positively.

A second trait is *trustworthiness*. A Christian leader is honest and transparent with all his dealings and relationships. A leader must be worthy of the trust of those who follow; he must be a man of integrity and a man of his word.

Third, the spiritual leader is *disciplined*. He is able to lead others because he has conquered himself — and has been conquered by Christ. The man of leadership caliber will work while others waste time, study while others sleep. He will pray while others play.

Fourth, a leader has *confidence*. If a leader does not believe in himself, no one else will.

A fifth trait is *decisiveness*. When all the facts are in, swift and clear decision is the mark of a true leader. He will resist the temptation to procrastinate in reaching a decision, and he will not vacillate ·after the decision has been made. Indecision in a time of emergency destroys the capacity to lead.

Sixth, *courage* marks strong leadership. Courage of the highest order is demanded of the spiritual leader. The highest degree of courage is seen in the person who is most fearful but refuses to capitulate to the fear. However fearful they might have been, God's leaders in every generation have been commanded to "be of good courage.'' Courage is the capacity to stay in there five minutes longer!

Humor is another vital trait of leadership. This is expressed in the ability to see the funny or strange side of life. It is reported that Admiral Chester W. Nimitz, upon viewing the devastation of Kwajalein after a battle in World War II, remarked to his staff, "It's the worst devastation I've ever seen except for that last Texas picnic in Honolulu." A good leader knows the value of a contagious smile.

A further trait of leadership — and so important — is *loyalty*, expressed in constancy, steadfastness, and faithfulness. A lack of loyalty to leadership will destroy an organization. As the group must be loyal to the leader, he in turn must be loyal to them.

A final trait (though there are many more that could be added) is *unselfishness*. This is demonstrated by that leader who can forget his own needs in the interests of others. Self-preservation is acknowledged to be the first law of nature, but self-sacrifice remains the greatest rule of grace, says Kenneth Wishart.

As expressed earlier, leadership usually is not something that a person is born with — it does not come naturally for most. Therefore it is vital that people striving to lead others take the necessary measures to learn the techniques and develop those traits which will enhance their effectiveness. Merely emulating someone else will not bring about the desired ends. Nor does leadership come in Ten Easy Steps. It can come about only by learning one's weaknesses, evaluating the hindrance to change and then utilizing this knowledge by putting it to work to develop the strengths to the maximum.

Any Difference for Christians?

What is true of the secular man as regards these traits is equally true of a Christian. His personality and feelings of himself can constitute success or failure. Contrary to what many Christians think, a Christian view of leadership does not automatically press a person into a prescribed mold. His Christian commitment and dedication should directly affect his motives and goals, but it will not necessarily prescribe his style or the methods he may employ to accomplish the task of molding people to an assigned task. This is so because of the individual differences to be found in people. Each leader brings to bear certain unique qualities, a certain character structure and capacity.

The Bible clearly points this out in Hebrews 11. The leaders mentioned there are as varied in characteristics as the situations required. A careful study of each person's personality will disclose the manifold diversity and ability of each and show that each had a high estimate of himself to believe that God had uniquely chosen him for a mission.

So one personality type as over against another does not guarantee success. In the final analysis it comes down to whether one is willing to pay the price and shoulder the responsibility to carry through the tasks given him.

Therefore it is impossible to find a consistent pattern of personality traits, because human behavior is so dynamic and complex. The measuring instruments cannot determine precisely what qualities are required at all times and at given times.

Having said this, it remains true that the personality of the leader plays a vital role to initiate change. Once the stage is set, the presence of an outstanding leader is indispensable. Without him there will be no movement. The ripeness of the times does not automatically produce a mass movement, nor can elections, laws, and administrative bureaucrats make one. It needs the iron will, daring, and vision of an exceptional leader to concert and mobilize existing attitudes and impulses into the collective drive of a mass movement.

The leader's personality is more often than not, then, what sparks the vision and enthusiasm and fuses diversity into unity. He has to kindle desire in others from his inner self, and that is why it is so important that he has a good, healthy ego.

The Christian leader should always be conscious of his committed responsibility to provide spiritual leadership. This means his personality will emit a quality about him that draws others to him. This attractiveness will show itself in his reasonableness, consideration, genuine love, and a forbearing spirit rather than in a contentious disposition.

He will seek to emulate the spirit of Christ through his personality. He will practice a congenial spirit and a gentleness that makes him hospitable and open to the needs of others.

The Christian leader should have the best feeling about himself because Christ has redeemed him and placed him in His forever family. A believer is a created workmanship of God (Eph. 2:8-10), precious in His sight. No Christian should grovel in the dust with weak feelings of self-worth. God thought enough of us to send His Son to die for us — that makes us pretty important!

Can Personality Be Changed?

Persons really in touch with themselves make the best leaders. If a leader senses he is immature or unstable, he should seek to improve himself. Personality cultivation helps to make an individual more personable and pleasant to be around; but he can reach this plateau only by being aware of and responsive to life situations. A legitimate question may be raised: Can personality be changed or achieved? Most psychologists agree that to a certain extent one's personality can change through emotional growth. Therefore personality cultivation can be achieved through training, therapy, and realistically facing one's deficiencies in relationships with people.

As one changes and enlarges his capacity to appreciate and relate to others, his personality is enriched. When this happens, the intellect and emotions become keener and more perceptive. The result is a warmer, more responsive, and aware human being who is in tune with others in his feelings.

Reading the excellent literature relating to emotional growth is one way to cultivate an enriched personality. Another is to take self-improvement courses that help a person develop poise and confidence. We hear much today about self-actualization from secular sources; the Christian leader must also come to grips with his need to develop his selfhood. He must learn how he comes across to other people through feedback from others. Nothing, however, can actually take the place of depth therapy that helps give a person insight into his own repressions, regressions, and emotional hang-ups.

If the person has the will, he can strengthen and enrich his personality by learning or relearning behavioral responses. He can learn to give up his defensiveness, learn to be himself without having to please people all the time, learn how to handle criticism, and gain the structure to cope better with anxiety and conflict.

This kind of perspective broadens greatly one's range of interests and provides more sensitivity to people's needs. It is infinitely satisfying and rewarding — and strengthens leadership.

The need for a clear grasp of leaders as persons is more than just an idea in a social psychology book. History discloses that successful people in all walks of life must recognize their own importance in terms of tasks performed. By the same token, leaders must have that inherent power of self-realization which motivated them to achieve beyond the average level.

We hear much today about psychocybernetics. Many Christians placed in positions of leadership would profit from taking a closer look at themselves to forge ahead toward personal goals. True self-realization is never a static situation; inner resources of power and drive must ever thrust him ahead in effective service for Christ. The self-concept of the strong leader, therefore, must ever evolve. Such a process helps one set goals and objectives, and this self-expectation allows a leader to search for unrealized power and find it.

Kenneth Gangel says that many ambitious men get nowhere

because of the weakness of their self-concept. This involves such key questions as "How do I view my life?" "What do I believe God wants to do with me?" "What are my values?" "What are my spiritual gifts?" "What are my lifetime goals?" "What does God have to change in my life in order for me to realize those goals?" He states,

> It is not my intent to make this sound like so much religious humanism. But self-actualization can, indeed, be an analysis of the realization of God-given gifts and capacities exercised through the power of the Holy Spirit and by means of the grace of the heavenly Father. Achievement does not have to be for selfish ends nor does it have to be attained through fleshly efforts.

> It seems to me that the apostle Paul is a shining example of the power of self-realization. A man who had achieved far beyond most of his peers, yet perennially dissatisfied with those achievements, he pressed on to higher levels of spiritual growth, wider outreach for the cause of the gospel, and a more significant and lasting impact on the lives of other men (Philippians 3:10-14).[2]

Most people have latent and undeveloped traits, which through lack of self-awareness and the consequent lack of self-knowledge may long remain undiscovered. J. Oswald Sanders supplies us with some suggested standards of self-measurement that can aid in the detection of weakness which would make one unfit for leadership.

> Have you ever broken yourself of a bad habit? To lead others, one must be master of oneself.

> Do you retain control of yourself when things go wrong? The leader who loses self-control in testing circumstances forfeits respect and loses influence. He must be calm in crises, and resilient in adversity and disappointment. . . .

> Can you handle criticism objectively and remain unmoved under it?

> Do you turn it to good account? The humble man can derive benefit from petty and even malicious criticism.

> Can you use disappointments creatively? . . .

> Do you possess the ability to secure discipline without having to resort to a show of authority? True leadership is an internal quality of the spirit and requires no external show of force.

> Have you qualified for the beatitude pronounced on the peace-maker? It is much easier to *keep* the peace than to *make* peace where it has been shattered. An important function in leadership is conciliation — the ability to discover common ground between opposing viewpoints and then induce both parties to accept it. . . .

> Can you induce people to do happily some legitimate thing which they would not normally wish to do?

Can you accept opposition to your viewpoint or decision without considering it a personal affront and reacting accordingly? Leaders must expect opposition and should not be offended by it.

Do you find it easy to make and keep friends? Your circle of loyal friends is an index of the quality and extent of your leadership.

Are you unduly dependent on the praise or approval of others? Can you hold a steady course in the face of disapproval and even temporary loss of confidence?

Are you at ease in the presence of your superiors or strangers?

Do your subordinates appear at ease in your presence? A leader should give an impression of sympathetic understanding and friendliness that will put others at ease.

Are you really interested in people? In people of all types and all races? Or do you entertain respect of persons? . . . An antisocial person is unlikely to make a good leader.

Do you possess tact? Can you anticipate the likely effect of a statement before you make it? . . .

Do you nurse resentments, or do you readily forgive injuries done to you? . . . [3]

A person may be quite aware of his deficiencies in these matters and others, but unless he does something about it, nothing is really gained. Concentrating on strengthening good points and correcting bad ones is essential. Cooperation with the working and ministry of the Holy Spirit within our lives, as well as self-analysis, will bring many positive, rewarding results.

THE REAL KEY TO PERSONALITY

Modern behavioral scientists and Christian psychologists confirm the fact that the "self-image" — a person's mental and spiritual picture of himself — is the real key to personality and behavior. All would agree that one is never too young or too old to change his self-image and thereby start a new life. Thousands of case histories show that people do change, sometimes very dramatically, but there is not a guaranteed formula that works for everyone because people respond to various approaches. One thing is certain: self-analysis is essential for a person to develop his psychological skills, for as one becomes more familiar with his own needs, he learns to understand other people as well.

In conclusion, then, personal development — dealing with attitudes, style, and personality — is one of the keys to outstanding and respected leadership. Development of potential qualities is the most promising way to increase overall effectiveness.

Notes

[1]Maxwell Maltz, *Psycho-Cybernetics* (Hollywood: Wilshire Publishing Co., 1960, 1964), pp. 110, 112.

[2]Kenneth Gangel, *Competent to Lead* (Chicago: Moody Press, 1974), pp. 122-23.

[3]J. Oswald Sanders, *Spiritual Leadership* (Chicago: Moody Press, 1967), pp. 26-28.

CHAPTER NINE

The Price
of Leadership

Every worthwhile accomplishment has a price tag in terms
of hard work, patience, faith, and endurance.

True leadership, even when it is practiced by the
most mature and emotionally stable person, always
exacts a toll on the individual. In our world it seems to be axiomatic
that the greater the achievement, the higher the price to be paid. The
same is true of leadership. Jesus Himself seemed to have this thought
in mind when He said, "If you really want to find your life, you must
lose it" (Luke 9:24).

It is so very true that any worthwhile accomplishment has a price
tag on it. The issue reduces itself to one basic question: How much are
you really willing to pay in hard work and sweat, in patience, in faith
and endurance to obtain it?

Ted Williams — baseball superstar of the forties and fifties, Hall
of Famer, and considered to be one of the greatest hitters ever to have
played the game — was known as a "natural" hitter. He was once
asked about his natural ability and immediately replied, "There is no
such thing as a natural born hitter. I became a good hitter because I
paid the price of constant practice, constant practice." To the casual
observer, the way he swung the bat made it look so easy. Likewise,
professional excellence in leadership doesn't just happen; it comes
about only through persistent effort.

Let us consider some aspects in which the cost is high for any person who is in a place of leadership or aspires to it.

CRITICISM

Criticism is a great price paid by leaders. If one cannot handle criticism, it means that basically he is emotionally immature. This defect will eventually show up and impede his and the group's progress toward the common goal. Every leader has to expect some of it. But it can work for the ultimate good if the leader is able to accept it.

I can see that often it has been those people who criticized me who helped me the most. How hard it was to take at the time, but how wonderfully redemptive such situations became! The only way we really get to know ourselves is by feedback from other people. We really don't know how we come across to people unless they tell us, so we need responses from them.

Backslappers help us feel better about ourselves, but we don't actually profit by them. Real change and emotional growth come by facing our weaknesses and personality defects as others see us. This is a price of leadership, because the leader is in a position of wider exposure. His visibility makes him more susceptible to criticism. But the mature leader is able to handle this and makes the needed personal adjustments and corrections. He is able to say, in essence, "Thank you for your criticism of my life. It has led me to a deeper self-examination, which I needed."

FATIGUE

Someone has said that the world is run by tired men. There is probably real substance in the statement, for genuine leaders must be willing to rise early and study longer than their contemporaries. Some men have tremendous stamina, but fatigue will frequently set in if they want to go somewhere with their organization and in their leadership responsibilities.

A wise leader will try to find a balance and seek an avocation, a change of pace, to reduce stress. He must seek some pleasurable recreation or he will eventually lose his usefulness. You have no doubt heard the cliche, "I'd rather burn out for God than rust out for the devil." The spirit of that is noble and pious-sounding, and a person's dedication must come close to the tenor of the thought. But on the other hand, if a person can learn how to relax and not spread himself too thin, his effectiveness will be magnified.

If a person "burns out" completely, his influence and contribution end. Proper health care, rest, and balance will help a leader maintain his ability to persist. But a leader must be prepared to recognize the toll upon him, both emotionally and physically.

Within weeks of writing this chapter, I fell prey to complete exhaustion while ministering overseas. I had to cut short my ministry abroad and come home for rest and a complete change of pace. Had I practiced months earlier what I now preach, this would never have happened. That "change of pace" is an absolute necessity for the hard-driving leader.

TIME TO THINK

Another price paid by Christian leaders is the time that must be taken for creative thinking and meditation. We do not often think of this as a price to pay, but it is. Most people are too busy to take time to really think.

For the sake of an objective, many leaders want to surge ahead without paying the price of thinking it through to determine the best methodology to meet the goal. It is well said that "the solution is not to work harder, but to work smarter."

Most successful ventures are achieved only after many hours of deep thinking and careful scrutiny.

LONELINESS

A fourth price the leader has to pay — one we seldom consider — is the willingness to be alone because he has lost his freedom in the service of others. A true leader, as we noted earlier, promotes others — their interests, values, and goals. At the same time, the effective leader must strive to fulfill his own potential and goals without being absorbed into the group. This leaves him living in a balance alone, somewhere in between, because he has to both identify with and be isolated from people.

All strong leaders become so because they are able to identify readily with people but not become "one of the boys." A leader has to be ready to walk away from the crowd and be alone. Jesus often did this in His ministry. Though the leader may be very friendly by nature, he must at times be prepared to tread a lonely path.

The leader must be able to welcome friendship, but he has to be mature enough and contain enough inner strength to stand alone even when there is much opposition as he performs his tasks.

Close scrutiny of Bible characters whom God so richly blessed and used discloses that more often than not they were men of solitude. The prophets, for example, were extremely lonely; they were often misunderstood, and they were threatening to people because of their direct rebukes of the people's behavior. Today as yesterday, the lonely preacher is the one who says "Thus saith the Lord" and calls people to repentance.

One reason loneliness is so difficult is that leaders may need people emotionally. Therefore they are unable to become private persons.

Another reason why loneliness is so difficult in leadership is because God made us social creatures. A basic drive of the human personality is the need for belonging and acceptance by our peers. It is only natural to want to be close to people and share the burdens of responsibility. It can be difficult to have to make decisions as a leader that greatly affect the lives of others. Leaders are often set apart: it is a great price they must pay.

IDENTIFICATION

Not only must the leader be alone and be isolated at times, but paradoxically he must also identify with the group. He must always remain ahead of the group, but simultaneously walk with the people he leads. This can be a fine line. There must be some distance between the leader and his followers. It is vital that the leader recognize this principle, yet be able to relate to his associates.

To be effective, the leader cannot run too far ahead of others. The Bible is filled with illustrations portraying the identification of leaders with people. The supreme example was our Lord Jesus, who often shared joy or sorrow with people. His suffering death on the Cross was the epitome of identification with mankind. The apostle Paul said he would become a Jew or a Greek or a slave in order to win each respective person (1 Cor. 9:19-23).

So, in a certain sense, the true leader has to pay the price of getting close, belonging to a group. This means he must be willing to be an open, honest human being. His humanness has to come through. He cannot be seen as a robot, a cold, mechanical person afraid of letting his true self emerge.

To identify with people, the leader must pay the price of taking time to know his people — to share in their emotions, victories, defeats. Since most goals cannot be reached in isolation, the group must be leaned upon. The leader has to be aware of the group-mind, be willing to make concessions, and lead graciously without losing sight of the long-range objective.

MAKE UNPLEASANT DECISIONS

Another price for the leader to pay when he gets to know or identify with his people is making the mandatory decisions that affect the ultimate good of an organization. Many times it becomes the duty of an effective leader to remove someone who is not performing up to the stated standard. Christian organizations often have trouble at this point because leaders are naturally loathe to hurt people.

But a person who constantly or consistently fails to perform with distinction is a hindrance to an organization's effectiveness. To let such a person retain his responsibility negatively affects others and hinders the progress and dynamic of the group.

All leaders must be willing to pay this price for the sake of the whole. It is not easy, especially when one desires approval from everyone.

In most cases, when a person is relieved because of unsatisfactory performance, he is being favored: when he is inadequate on a job, he is slowly destroyed inside by the pressure and strain. Secretly he may be praying for deliverance!

COMPETITION

Still another peril of leadership is the effect of competition. Lest we consider this a bad term, we must remember that competition is the genius that made America great. Without it, man would have little drive to achieve. With it, especially in the economic sphere, the consumer is protected, because it helps to keep thieves out of the market and guarantees quality at lower prices.

But there is a price for leaders to pay if they suffer from a "competition anxiety" that takes the form of either the fear of failure or the fear of success.

The fear of failure stifles competition because the leader will be afraid to proceed or get too involved; achievement is curtailed, and a loss of identity is sustained. To overcome this anxiety, the leader must do some serious reality-testing to know what the competitive world really is, not what his illusions tell him. He must change his own self-concept in accordance with rational standards.

The fear of success can be just as crippling. The leader may appear to be highly adjusted, outgoing, and extroverted, but the price paid by an organization with such people is very high. A leader with this kind of neurosis will develop increasing guilt feelings as he and the organization achieve. This kind of person may strive hard, but will usually falter before the actual achievement. He will often find some excuse (which to him is perfectly logical) to block the realization of the ultimate goal.

In a Christian organization, unless it is involved in product sales, competition should be played down because a rival spirit is contrary to strengthening the body of Christ. We are told that in honor we are to prefer or exalt the other person (Rom. 12:10).

With this one exception, the leader must keep his competitive edge sharp. Only in this way can he lead effectively to achieve the goals.

ABUSE OF POWER

In the long history of mankind, power has become accepted as a basic characteristic of leadership. In any organization, including a Christian group, when a person is given authority he is in a legitimate position to exercise control and influence. For some people this is ego-building and leads to autocracy. It is a peril, and there is a price to pay to keep from falling prey to this insidious temptation.

FALSE PRIDE AND JEALOUSY

False pride and jealousy are twins. Popularity can affect a leader's performance. Feelings of infallibility and indispensability can decrease his effectiveness. And it is not uncommon for leaders to go through deep depression.

Every person must have some pride. It is good to be proud of some achievement; it is good to be proud of our children for good behavior or performance; it is healthy to be proud of our husband or wife. But pride turns to egotism when we magnify ourselves to the point at which we have no place for the other person. It is false pride when we become wrapped up in ourselves to the degree that other people count for little. This must be guarded against. This kind of pride or egotism is far different from having a healthy self-concept. The latter person is balanced in his appraisal of others and himself.

The leader who has long been admired is especially susceptible to this peril. He may overact when others are promoted, exonerated, or selected for certain assignments he expected. Jealousy is then the fruit. He becomes suspicious of rivals.

An exaggerated deference to leaders can lead to a personality cult. When a leader succumbs to the temptation of popularity, it can become a fierce problem because his popularity can get in the way of performance. A leader is more effective if he can point people to the group or organization he leads. Loyalty must be to the group first. The Christian leader must point people to Christ rather than to himself.

We all desire to be popular, and there is no great virtue in being unpopular. But there must be balance. A leader should be respected and held in esteem to get the job done better, but popularity can be purchased at too high a price.

When the price of humility is not paid, the temptations of infallibility and indispensability lurk. When people have false pride, it is easy to accept the rationalization that they are less liable to make mistakes than others. Unless a person perceives his true self-worth and is led by the Holy Spirit, he may easily fall into this subtle trap. Despite experience and maturity, leaders often fail to see that all of us are prone to make mistakes. "After all, my judgment has usually proved accurate," is what many reply.

The leader must have convictions and know what he believes, but that is quite different from the infallibility illusion. Leaders who project this notion cannot be respected for very long by their followers.

Closely allied to infallibility is the feeling that one is irreplaceable. Some leaders feel their organization cannot survive without them, and they cling to authority as long as they can. This is a peril because development and progress can be held up for years when the mantle should have been passed on to some younger or better qualified person.

The myth of indispensability is often perpetuated by the best-intentioned people. Frequently organizations face this with their older leaders, who become progressively less able with age to assess their contributions objectively, who may drag their heels and really unconsciously hinder — or at least retard — growth and development.

UTILIZATION OF TIME

Of all the things we have to work with, the most important is the time God has given to us. There is a price to pay in the use of our time because it seems that we human beings are born congenitally lazy. So we have to alter this process.

In the final analysis, managing our time really means managing ourselves. We have to budget our time just as carefully as we have to budget our money.

It is a liberating thought that time can be a tool to be used to good advantage. Given two leaders of equal ability, the one who uses best this tool by planning his time more effectively will far outperform the other person. He will take time for creative thinking and the problem-solving which is vital to the job. The other simply puts them off until he "finds" time.

How often we hear, "I wish I knew how to manage my time better." Rarely do we hear, "I wish I knew how to manage myself better," but that's really what it comes down to. This will be discussed more fully in the next chapter.

REJECTION

A leader, especially a Christian, must also be ready to pay the price of personal rejection. There is always the strong possibility that somewhere he may be maligned for his faith or Christian perspective on issues. This was the path that Jesus walked: "He came unto His own but they received Him not" (John 1:11).

The leader must be able at times to resist praise. He must have courage to be willing to stand up against the spirit of the age. He puts praise of God above the praise of men. He knows that "the fear of man lays a snare" (Prov. 29:25 RSV). The verdicts or judgments of men do not change his standard if it is truly God- and people-oriented.

It takes a person with good ego strength to be able to cope with rejection. Normal, well-adjusted people want to be liked; it can become a difficult road to walk if a leader feels the cooling winds of indifference or dislike. Often people who are rejected are not recognized for their strength until they have left or died. Monuments are then built with the stones once thrown at him in life. This is not easy to accept, but the leader must be prepared emotionally and spiritually to face this possibility.

To help overcome rejection, the leader must be taught as a disciple, leaning upon Christ. He may in moments of loneliness or isolation feel disappointment or rejection. But he will use these moments of depression to challenge and arouse new creative thoughts to stimulate him to go on toward a more realistic appraisal, perhaps, of the temporary situation.

In order to face these feelings, he must be constrained by God's love which motivates him. The true leader knows that the driving force in his life is none other than the Christ who motivated the apostle John to say, "He who is in you is greater than he who is in the world" (1 John 4:4 RSV). As a disciple, then, the Christian leader is motivated by love for others and is thus willing to accept rejection for the cause of Christ, who was Himself willing to do "the will of Him that sent me."

You may be able to think of other ways in which a true leader must be ready to pay a price if he is to retain a responsible position. When all is said and done, when he is willing to pay the sacrifices necessary for success, his span of service will be marked by high quality and excellence.

CHAPTER TEN

The Measurements of Leadership

Leadership excellence demands a passion for efficiency and a high level of performance.

President John F. Kennedy said in several of his speeches that success hinges upon a "passion for excellence." In every sphere of human activity this tends to be a missing quality. Whether it be in the secular, business world or in church-related fields, far too many are content to settle for mediocrity in effectiveness and results. This creates all kinds of tension, dissipation of manpower, economic losses, and frequently total failure. As we focus on the topic of excellence, we do well to grasp the depth of insight inherent in this statement by Samuel Logan Brengle:

> One of the outstanding ironies of history is the utter disregard of ranks and titles in the final judgments men pass on each other. The final estimate of men shows that history cares not an iota for the rank or title a man has borne, or the office he has held, but only the quality of his deeds and the character of his mind and heart.

Christian organizations need to give special attention to this matter of excellence. Nearly all of them attach some nebulous kind of spiritual aura to performance, workmanship, and attitudes. Because they more or less feel it is a matter between the worker and the Lord, they often fail to demand excellence and challenge employees to strive for it.

Therefore we find in a high percentage of Christian agencies and organizations no such thing as quality control. The assumption in churches, for example, is that the work is being done by lay volunteers, thus not so many demands should be made. "Some work or inferior work is better than none" goes the rationalization. So most groups dare not have a high expectation level of performance. A leader must be committed to high efficiency and quality in himself and in his subordinates. Mediocrity cannot be his mode.

No organization on the face of the earth should resist shoddy work more than a Christian service. I have concluded that it is not better programs, but people who build quality.

How's Your Attitude?

I have discovered that attitudes as much as anything else erode quality. Many of the problems people have are self-induced. Excellence in leadership cannot be achieved when there are attitudinal blocks. Following are some helpful suggestions to improve or change your or your people's attitudes:

1. Our attitude at the beginning of a task will affect its successful outcome more than anything else.
2. Our attitude toward life determines life's attitude toward us.
3. Our attitude toward others will determine their attitude toward us.
4. Before a person can achieve the kind of life he wants, he must think, act, walk, talk, and conduct himself in all of his affairs as would the person he wishes to become.
5. The higher you go in any organization of value, the better the attitude you'll find.
6. Hold successful, positive thoughts in your mind.
7. Always make a person feel needed, important, and appreciated and they will return the same to you.
8. Part of a good attitude is to look for the best in new ideas and look for good ideas everywhere.
9. Don't broadcast personal problems. It probably won't help you, and it cannot help others.
10. Don't talk about your health unless it is good.
11. Radiate the attitude of well-being, of confidence of a person who knows where he is going.
12. Treat everyone with whom you come in contact as highly and beautifully important.

Let us note several important factors that help us define excellence in leadership. These are some measurements, guidelines, and personal traits needed for high and successful performance.

Performance

Performance is the first indicator, because competence determines the level of operation for any organization. Competence is an early separator of men from boys. People are seldom placed in leadership positions and given the accompanying status without first displaying real ability in a given area. It is competence that gives a person his first raise and promotion, and it is competence that provides the impetus for moving up the ladder.

When a person demonstrates this competence, his chance of promotion to a supervisory position is much greater. If he shows he can handle skillfully the authority that goes with position, then his superiors know he can make the grade. Competence is probably the one ingredient the group looks for more than any other in determining leadership positions.

When a person is selected to lead, he must continue to cultivate breadth and depth of excellence in competence. When this takes place, confidence will be exuded, which in turn rubs off on others. If, for example, you wish to see a certain proposal of yours adopted by the organization, you had better lead from competence. If — after analyzing and putting together all the pertinent information, facts, and figures — you are able to evolve a case so complete, watertight, and incontrovertible that the sheer weight of the confidence of your arguments in the proposal carries the day, even if your superiors may be in a most critical and skeptical mood, you are leading from a sense of competence.

Competence also includes the ability to see the defects and weaknesses in a proposal and to anticipate objections before they are raised. Touching base with them gives others the feeling that you have thought through well the total plan. Being unprepared destroys the confidence people have in leadership and undermines authority and influence.

This means you will not lead from one component to camouflage a weakness in another. That would be somewhat like a preacher I heard about: he had written in the margin of his sermon manuscript, "Argument weak here; speak loudly."

We have all had the experience of dealing with a person who wants to see something done, and done now. In industry it might be illustrated by a person who comes to you for a decision requiring a great deal of technical competence. Since that person may have much expertise in the matter, he may try to "snow" you; he has done much homework on the project with infinite details. As you begin to listen, you get lost in the technicalities until you see that it is way over your head. Of course you don't want him to know that, so when pressed for a decision you simply defer the decision to another time with the comment, "I need more information or more time to think on this."

When asked why, you say, "Well, because that's my decision." The person now begins to recognize that you have substituted your authority of position for that of competence. In army terms it could be said, "You've pulled your rank."

Again, this point may be illustrated by a group in a conference debating a certain issue. The leader may find that he holds to a minority position with his back to the wall. When pressed for an opinion he may reply that he is against the proposal on the basis of principle. This evasion only aggravates people the more. Eventually communication and confidence begin to break down, and the conference ends in a deadlock. The leader consoles himself by the rationalization that the early Christians died for the sake of conviction and principles; but without realizing it, he is defending against a deficiency in his personality.

What is stubbornness in children is seen as strength in adulthood. The person who is unable to face conflict loses much of the authority his character would give to him. This person's problem is that he cannot really stand up to his convictions and disagree on a mature level.

There can be no substitute for competent leadership. Someone has well said, "There is no automatic transmission in any group to make it run. . . . There has to be someone who knows how to work it to make it go."

EFFICIENCY

High levels of performance are always marked by efficiency in charting organizational direction. The best leaders always have a course charted, goals determined, and objectives described. They have in mind the direction they want, and they realize that specific goals are needed to achieve the ultimate objective. This means the leader must be able to set specific objectives. This requires keen knowledge and insight.

It is wisdom that provides the ability to use knowledge with sound judgment and discernment (Phil. 1:9). So wisdom is more than just the accumulation of facts. It is insight into the heart of things. Every leader should seek this quality because it helps to be delivered from himself. It imparts the necessary balance and delivers him from extravagance and eccentric idiosyncracies.

EFFECTIVENESS

Another measure of excellence is effectiveness. This will improve as the leader sets down his priorities and the proper allocation of time. As indicated in the chapter on the personality of the leader, one must take measures to develop himself. To excel ought to be the dominant expectation of all those who lead. This means they constantly must strive for a proper balance between what is urgent and what is important. General Eisenhower undoubtedly was correct when he said, "The urgent is seldom important, and the important is seldom urgent."

I have known executives who approach golf or skiing or tennis with more intense effort than they approach their task as leaders. Excellence requires more than reading a book on management principles. Professional expertise demands that we take continual action for improvement. Here are several steps suggested by my friend Frank Goble in his helpful book *Excellence in Leadership*.

I will reserve the following dates and times for an improvement program.

_____

_____

I will schedule a meeting with my staff to plan an organizational improvement program. Who? When? Where?

_____

_____

I will start holding regular meetings with my staff as the first step toward adopting the coordinated team approach at all levels under my jurisdiction. Who? When? Where?

_____

_____

I will attend some seminars. Which seminars? When?

_____

_____

I will start reading leadership literature. What? When?

_____

_____

I will start a leadership library. How? When? Where?

_____

_____

I will obtain and display some signs to remind me and my associates to do things in a professional way.

I will analyze my own use of time. This is how I will proceed:

I will seek a qualified consultant to help improve personal and organizational effectiveness. Who? When?

The area which shows the greatest possibility for improvement is:

I will start there. What? How? When?

I will do the following:

[1]

This checklist is a tool to identify those areas needing improvement. The list can and should be expanded and adapted to your individual needs.

Priorities can never become a reality without the proper use of time. Excellence in any field is crippled or thwarted without it. Therefore, we need to give more attention to this vital subject.

Peter Drucker states in his book *The Effective Executive* that effective leaders *know* where their time goes. They work systematically at managing it by setting priorities, and they stay with these priority decisions.

Time in itself is really not the problem, but people who use it are. People who excuse their failures by saying "I don't have time" really are admitting to mismanagement of time.

Every leader should consider how he estimates the worth of time. As an analogy we should treat it exactly as if it were money, for it requires the investment of our energy to bring forth profitable results. It goes without saying that time spent improving personal procedures will reap great dividends.

Notes

[1]Frank Goble, *Excellence in Leadership* (New York: American Management Association, 1972), pp. 183-84.

CHAPTER ELEVEN

Personal Traits in Leadership

The primary qualification for successful leadership is personal integrity.

To attain excellence, I believe all the traits cited in this chapter are absolutely essential. In my mind they stand out because they have proved to provide the stimulus and means to reach the highest plateaus of success.

DESIRE FOR ACHIEVEMENT

Ambition may be called by many names: motivation, drive, enthusiasm, or the hope for achievement. Regardless, it is essential because it is fundamental if a person is to be a self-starter. Otherwise he must content himself with being a follower rather than a leader.

Ambition must be realistic. Some people set impossible goals for themselves. Being overzealous, they drive themselves to complete exhaustion or thorough frustration, which may lead to a neurotic depression.

A man who has fixed purposes and goals knows where he is going. He will accomplish so much more than the person without clearly defined goals. Leaders get their greatest satisfaction from accomplishing goals; they are always looking for new worlds to conquer. They usually have strong egos, and their feelings of self-esteem and self-respect must be satisfied through their own and the group's expression. How important it is for the leader to have committed these drives to the Savior! Leaders seem to have one common denominator: restless, curious, and exploring minds coupled with determination to achieve.

Ambition is so important because it is self-sustaining and contagious if it is not faked. The true leader is emotionally primed with the power to summon and elevate the desires of others above a merely rational level. Such feelings, of course, must issue from a sense of the importance of the purpose. To the Christian leader, his highest ambition must be to bring honor and glory to Christ, with his drives and ambitions controlled by the Holy Spirit.

It must be remembered that our influence will be determined in large part by our zeal. If one lacks enthusiasm, perhaps he should take a close look at his personality structure as well as his basic faith or life outlook; the pessimist or cynic is never an enthusiastic person.

Someone has said that enthusiasm serves as the jet fuel that will lead one to blast off into unexcelled achievements.

ACCEPTANCE OF AUTHORITY

Excellence in leadership requires a strong sensitivity to using authority at just the right time. This pays off in a leader's ability to bring about change in a group or a person. When a person can make the proper judgments, he can motivate or act in a certain way at a certain time. It is this ability that constitutes one's authority to manage.

But first we have to understand authority. A common but well-reasoned definition is this: "Authority is whatever you possess at the moment that causes someone else to do what you want him to do at the moment." In other words, any leader who is able to get done what he wants has all the authority he needs at the moment.

A journal issued by the California Institute of Technology in October 1970 and written by William Oncken, Jr., says that authority comprises four components.

1. The Authority of Competence: The more competent the other fellow knows you are, the more confident he will be that you know what you are talking about and the more likely he will be to follow your orders, requests, or suggestions. He will think of you as an authority in the matter under consideration and will feel it risky to ignore your wishes. If he does not have this confidence he will, at best, give you lip service or, at worst, ignore you or sabotage you.

2. The Authority of Position: This component gives you the right to tell someone "Do it or else." It has teeth. "The boss wants it" is a bugle call that can snap many an office or shop into action. His

position carries authority that demands deference. Only the "gambler" will capriciously ignore it.

3. The Authority of Personality: The easier it is for the other fellow to talk to you, to listen to you, or to work with you, the easier he will find it to respond to your wishes. The harder you are to do business with, the harder it will be for him to find satisfaction in doing what you want him to do. He already has one full-time problem — to succeed in his own job. If, in addition, he finds you difficult to talk to, listen to, or work with, he has two full-time problems. If both combined are too much for him he will not solve either problem well. At worst, he may fail at solving the first problem because he is too preoccupied with the second. In that event he certainly will not be doing what you want him to do. If, on the other hand, he has no "second problem," he may do more than you expected. It takes a lot of effort to say "no" to someone with whom it is easy to do business.

4. The Authority of Character: This component is your "credit rating" with other people as to your integrity, reliability, honesty, loyalty, sincerity, personal morals, and ethics. Obviously you will get more and better action from a man who has respect for your character than from one who hasn't. He acquires this respect (or lack of it) from the trail you leave behind you of promises kept or broken, expectations fulfilled or forgotten, statements corroborated or shown to be false. You get no credit for being truthful when it costs you nothing to tell the truth, for being honest when it costs you nothing to be honest, for being dependable when it costs you nothing to be dependable.

The measure other people place upon your character is how far you have been willing to put yourself out to maintain your record of honesty and dependability. This tells them at once how far they will want to put themselves out for you when the chips are down. The greater their respect, the farther they'll go, and the greater is the component of character in your overall authority.[1]

To get subordinates to act upon your desires, you need to demonstrate all four of these qualities. A leader who complains that he has responsibility without authority must be made aware that he can strengthen these segments of his life to gain more authority. To use the excuse that he "could get more done if he had more authority" is suspect, because he can always do something about it. Competence can be acquired, personality can be developed, and character can surely be cultivated.

Excellence is found in leadership only where a person will make those sacrifices to improve and strengthen himself. Then his authority will be used in the proper way and there will be a dynamic result from the overall group effort.

SELF-DISCIPLINE

Because we have devoted a whole chapter to motivation, only a passing reference is needed here to say that it is a prerequisite for leadership excellence. To control others, a person must have self-control. This is a crucial quality, for only the well-disciplined person can scale the heights. Through experience he has learned to handle the necessary rigors, sacrifices, and demands.

Many people have particular and unused gifts, both spiritual and natural, but either scorn authority or shirk the discipline to attain. Thus they quit along the way. The effective leader is one willing to work while others sleep, play, or waste time. He also constantly evaluates his abilities — and his weaknesses!

CREATIVITY

Individuals who have most indelibly influenced their generation are those who have had vision and the powers of creativity. Initiative is involved. Creative thinking simply means the ability to do original thinking. It is taking imagination and organizing it through self-initiated plans. The creative leader gleans ideas from many sources and integrates them until they become a finished product.

Creative thinking is not daydreaming, but a deliberate attempt to objectify mental activity. Psychologists say the creative art can become a habit by the person's working at it.

Many firms and Christian ministries today encourage a free exchange of ideas. This is called "brainstorming" or going into the "think tank." Leaders must take the lead in actually programming this into their enterprises.

Arnold Toynbee, assessing the flow of history, concluded that the rise and fall of societies has depended almost exclusively upon the quality of leadership. He believed it is the creative people who successfully help the advance of civilization.

DELEGATION

We will be discussing delegation in detail. We note that a good leader need not employ authoritarian measures to get the work done. The opposite method is delegation: a leader allows people under him to function responsibly in a given task. Excellence in leadership cannot be sustained when a manager feels he must do it all himself.

This is succinctly stated in a pamphlet, "How to Delegate Effectively," published by the Dartnell Corporation. In it Clarence B. Randall says,

The capacity for the delegation of authority and responsibility with just the right touch is a rather rare quality. Many men pride themselves upon possessing it who in fact do it badly.

I know a man who honestly believes that this is one of his strong points, but this is the situation as I have it from one of his associates. On Monday he calls in a subordinate, explains the problem, and tells him to get into it at once; on Tuesday he delegates it to another; on Wednesday he does the job himself and tells neither of the others that he has acted.

I know another executive who delegates all right — he never does anything himself if it can be avoided — but never in accordance with any discernible pattern; it is usually the first man he meets as he walks down the hall to whom he hands the file.

There is one final test, in my opinion, by which it can be determined whether an executive is objective and consistent in the practice of delegating authority, and that is this: if he can turn a job over to a junior and then support him in carrying it out in a manner quite different from that which he himself would have chosen, then he understands.

The fine art of delegating isn't as easy as just drawing a chart with vertical and horizontal lines that tie either jobs or people together, or even drafting a precise and detailed description of duties, for as often as not it works out that such documents serve to limit initiative rather than promote it. When too much emphasis is placed upon job definition, a junior is apt to think more about the limits of his authority than upon his opportunity, and hold back in fear of transgressing instead of plunging ahead with a bold course of action.

Delegation implies control, and that likewise calls for deft skill. The organization must be kept on the beam, and the effort of all must be directed toward a common end, yet the widest latitude which will not defeat that purpose must be permitted for the play of individual deviation in order that the drive that comes from enthusiasm may be maintained. "Doin' what comes naturally" is an important thing to foster in team play, for the man who does it his own way may do it better and faster than if he does it the way that would appeal to the boss. On rare occasions control must be absolute, and then the executive must be firm.

A good administrator not only learns to delegate authority but he also seeks to share his thinking with as many others as possible. This is not an easy habit for some men to acquire, however. Strong characters, in particular, tend to regard thinking as their prerogative . . . only.

(Pp. 12-13)

DECISIVENESS

A person who equivocates and vacillates, unable to stick with a decision, is not a good leader. To help lead others, a person must know what he wants and how to accomplish it. If it is difficult for him to make decisions, employees will lose faith and confidence in him and begin to question his ability. This undermines the defined objectives and policies of an organization.

When a leader is sure of the will of God and the right course of action, he is able immediately to make a decision regardless of the circumstances. The great leaders of the Bible seldom procrastinated in reaching a decision, nor did they vacillate after it had been made.

An authentic leader will gather as much information as necessary, accepting and respecting the opinions of others. Yet the time always comes when he must act decisively regardless of the disagreeing views. This means that he seizes the reins when necessary because he has a strong sense of his own destiny and has a certainty about the direction in which he should go.

Of tomorrow's many tasks, which deserve priority? The problem is, who decides — we ourselves, or the pressures? If pressures decide, then the important tasks will be predictably sacrificed. There will be no time for the most time-consuming part of any task, i.e., the conversion of decision into action.

Someone must make the new task his own. Passing the buck has no part in leadership excellence. The leader must therefore objectively and arbitrarily impose priorities. Remember, the pressures always favor yesterday rather than today and tomorrow. Pressures also favor what goes on inside the organization rather than outside it.

We should also remember that setting priorities really is not difficult. The harder task is setting what I call "posteriorities" — deciding what tasks *not* to tackle and sticking to the decision. Note that what one postpones, one usually abandons, or else takes it up later when the timing is wrong. Of course, setting a posteriority is always difficult because it is bound to be someone else's top priority. So what is needed here is courage to make firm decisions.

PERSISTENCE

Firmness of conviction is a vital quality for leadership excellence. Every success story that depicts the "log cabin to the White House" also contains the element of individual effort. These people never let defeat daunt them, though faced with severe tests and incredible obstacles.

Napoleon Hill, who studied the lives of many successful people, stated, "I had the happy privilege of analyzing both Mr. Edison and Mr. Ford, year by year, over a long period of years, and therefore the opportunity to study them at close range, so I speak from actual knowledge when I say that I found no quality save persistence, in either one of them, that even remotely suggested the major source of their stupendous achievements."[2]

Persistence must be balanced with great patience, because cherished plans often require much time to be implemented and fulfilled.

Courage is necessary for a leader to stand by his convictions and be persistent. Men and women of leadership qualities in the Bible were always individuals who demonstrated courage.

Someone has made this distinction between courage and persistence: "Courage is the desire to begin, and persistence is the desire to continue." A major reason why people lack courage is their fear of failure. This is an attitude of the mind fostered by infantile insecurity feelings. Perhaps as children they were many times laughed at or put down when they failed. This destroyed incentive and the desire to try again. Such traumas may greatly affect adult behavior and destroy the courage needed if leaders are to be successful. Courage is often simply the ability to "hang in there" five minutes longer.

Such a quality enables men to meet danger or difficulty with firmness. It helps them to face unpleasant tasks and even devastating facts and conditions. They are able to make firm decisions even when they know they will prove to be unpopular.

Certainly one of the greatest leaders of the century was Sir Winston Churchill, who never flinched from telling his people the truth, even when the truth was utterly distressing. Someone said of him, "I doubt if any man in history has ever made such grim utterances, yet given his people such a feeling of strength and exuberance — even cheerfulness." It was indeed his great courage and persistence in leadership that won the day for Britain at a supreme crisis moment in her history.

A BALANCED LIFE

A whole book could be written just on the theme of a balanced life. For a leader to excel, he must find avocations and interests in his life away from his job. He must not only provide materially for his family, but give them much of himself as well. I have found that excellence in leadership demands that the leader give his family priority over the long haul. Has your profession been capturing most of your time, stealing even those few moments you meant to invest in living life together with those you love?

I know a man whose boss, almost every time he saw him, would say, "Dave, is your family getting any of you? What about your family?" That man had the right perspective and with it a happy staff.

A person can become a "work-a-holic" by overcommitting himself financially, by making unrealistic plans, or simply by failing to recognize a personality defect. Often he may use work as an escape mechanism. Thus he has to drive himself to the exclusion of what should be his priorities.

It is most unfortunate that we deplore drug and alcoholic addicts but somehow promote and admire the work addict. We give him status and accept his estimate of himself. And all the while his family may be getting so little of his time and energy that they hardly know him.

Overwork is not the disease itself. It is the symptom of a deeper problem — of tension, of inadequacy, of a need to achieve that may have neurotic implications. Unfortunately for the work-a-holic, he has no home; his house is only a branch office. He won't take a vacation, can't relax, dislikes weekends, can't wait for Monday, and continues to make his own load heavier by bringing more work on himself. Such a person also is usually defending against having to get close to people.

We have all heard of leaders of corporations and businesses who have given their wives everything materially, but nothing of themselves. And thus comes a divorce because the husband-father is interested only in his work. But that hardly dissuades him. He reasons, "I can always get another wife, but where would I ever find another job like this one?" Such tragedies abound in our nation.

A person like this cannot remain successful, because sooner or later life will break down for him. His problem is priorities; it is a matter of basic values being askew. Remember always that your work or ministry or position dare never keep you from your family. If you fail them, you fail your greatest responsibility — and you are a failure in life.

FAITH AND PRAYER

For the Christian leader, faith and prayer are his vital breath because they touch infinite extremes that reach God Himself. Prayer cleanses, and it provides assurance and encouragement for the leader to press on. This is an art not taught by some reasoned philosophy; it is learned and developed only by the doing of it. Our Lord Jesus Himself and the apostle Paul are sufficient examples setting forth the supreme value of these spiritual exercises. The eminence of great leaders of the Bible is attributed to their greatness in prayer. Paul admonishes us in Ephesians 6:18 to give ourselves wholly to prayer.

Because leadership is the ability to move and influence people, the Christian leader must be alert to the most effective means of doing this. Often men become severe roadblocks to progress, and only God can change or remove the problem. Therefore leaders must rely upon God in prayer. To move men, the leader must be able to prevail upon

God. And prevailing prayer is the outcome of a right relationship with Him.

J. Donald Phillips, former president of Hillsdale College in Michigan, summarizes excellence in his "Credo For Management" printed in the college "Leadership Letter" of April 1964.

I BELIEVE that basic integrity is the primary qualification for successful management.

I BELIEVE that people, not products, are the real competitive difference between organizations, or companies.

I BELIEVE that management of people must begin with management of self.

I BELIEVE that the right to dignity and sense of worth is the intended heritage of every American.

I BELIEVE that free people should be persuaded, educated, trained, but not ordered . . . that all men at times will be subordinate but that none should be asked to be subservient.

I BELIEVE that human problems involve emotions and attitudes more significant and more persuasive than reason and logic, therefore I believe that communication begins with emotion, feeling and attitude — not with words.

I BELIEVE that decision making is best when encouraged at the level of the operation involved . . . that top management is often too far removed to hear the overtones which are often as important as fact.

I BELIEVE that delegation of authority must always follow delegation of responsibility.

I BELIEVE that most problems have many adequate solutions, and that some could be as good as my own or possibly even better.

I BELIEVE that job descriptions and job-execution interviews are good when used to dignify — but have the potential of being restrictive, confining and generally degrading.

I BELIEVE that danger is imminent when caution, orderliness and tested procedures replace the reasonable risk, adventure and experimentation which built the organization.

I BELIEVE that the profit motive and incentive are the privileges of management to be proudly exercised and proudly proclaimed . . . that the truth about our profits is far more favorable than the usual rumor and therefore that public and employee education programs concerning competitive enterprise is a positive responsibility of management.

I BELIEVE that it is my privilege and responsibility to see to it that each member of my group experiences democratic leadership . . . recognizes it as such . . . finds it emotionally satisfying . . . and finds it productive.

I BELIEVE that the responsibility of my management extends beyond my business into the building of my people toward becoming increasingly responsible American citizens and leaders in home, community, state and nation.

These things I believe for the good of the people of my company, for my company and for my country!

Sometime ago I came across an uncopyrighted pamphlet that included the following statement.

THE WORLD NEEDS MEN . . .

who cannot be bought;
whose word is their bond;
who put character above wealth;
who possess opinions and a will;
who are larger than their vocations;
who do not hesitate to take chances;
who will not lose their individuality in a crowd;
who will be as honest in small things as in great things;
who will make no compromise with wrong;
whose ambitions are not confined to their own selfish desires;
who will not say they do it ''because everybody else does it'';
who are true to their friends through good report and evil report, in adversity as well as in prosperity;
who do not believe that shrewdness, cunning and hardheadedness are the best qualities for winning success;
who are not ashamed or afraid to stand for the truth when it is unpopular, who can say ''no'' with emphasis, although all the rest of the world says ''yes.''

Notes

[1]Circular No. 36, "The Authority to Manage," by William Oncken, Jr. (Dallas: The William Oncken Corp., October 1970).

[2]Napoleon Hill, *Think and Grow Rich* (Greenwich, Conn.: Fawcett Publishers, Inc., 1958), p. 164.

CHAPTER TWELVE

Developing Leadership Skills

The death knell of any organization is to defy the need for raising the skill level of its people.

The development of leadership skills is a never-ending process. It is a continuous achievement which flows like a swollen river. The person who seemingly has achieved leadership must realize that he never "arrives." Simply learning some basic skills through a training course does not always — or even often — bring the best results. One must recognize that basic changes are required at times. The leader may be faced with the fact that he will need to revise his attitude or change his ambitions.

A GAUGE IS NEEDED

It is well said that leaders *learn* to be leaders. This means that time must be allowed for learners to develop. Before this can happen a group must have some kind of plan to find the best prospects. Random selection seldom brings good results, for if a person really has no potential ability, he should not be considered. Prospects should display some positive attitudes toward the group and give some strong evidence that he will be able to learn a new task that requires greater skill. Recognition of leadership ability is vital.

Among other things to look for is character. The ethics practiced by a person are a good measure of one's character. This includes the ability to make proper decisions, to know whether a course of action is morally right or wrong.

Personality is also important. A person being sought for leadership must be able to get along with people and be willing to cooperate in joint ventures.

Close scrutiny will uncover those individuals who appear to have greater native ability than others. When they are found it might be wise to assign them duties which are not too critical or vital. As they develop, the measure of responsibility may be expanded. If they seem to be able to follow through, this may measure potential as well as the ability to initiate action when decision is called for. A self-starting individual often shows leadership potential because this reveals motivation; it means he discerns the situation and then selects the best course of action.

Leadership potential requires some form of measurement. The following is a suggested list.[1]

1. Can he learn to carry out assignments?
2. Is he in harmony with group goals?
3. Is he compatible with others in the group?
4. Can he "tell" people what and how to do things?
5. Does he take orders without resentment or resistance?
6. Is he organized?
7. Does he feel responsibility?

Once the field has been researched, selection of the potential leaders should be made quickly.

The death knell of any organization, Christian or secular, is to defy the need for training of its more qualified people with potential. Unfortunately most training is directed more to a person's gaining skills than to the ability to influence others through leadership. Both are needed for a wholesome, balanced approach to get the maximum results.

Once people with evident potential are chosen, the first step in leadership training is always — without fail — the need for organizing the administration of leadership. A competent person, well respected and accepted, must be in charge of the plan. If possible, he should be a top executive who has this assigned responsibility, even if no formal training has been created.

Tests Are Needed

At the outset, potential leaders should be screened through the use of intelligence and psychological tests. More and more, Christian organizations are using these measures with good results. For example, many mainline denominations and faith mission societies in the United States put their missionary candidates through a battery of psychological tests. The added burden most Americans face when they go to foreign countries — lower standards of living from what they're used to, more expensive situations, separation from family and friends, financial burdens, learning new customs and languages — requires individuals to be sound emotionally along with having spiritual credentials. Nearly everyone experiences "culture shock." Statistics indicate there are far fewer psychological casualties having to return home now when good and proven testing materials are faithfully used.

Today as never before the field of testing is developed to disclose a person's normal and abnormal responses and motives. Such tests focus directly on problem areas and minimize lost time, trial and error, and bungling. For example, it is much better to see how people respond and behave to certain circumstances or stimuli in simulated situations than in actual events. Such readings can save an organization thousands of dollars and fruitless years of an applicant's career.

To ignore such a body of knowledge is foolish, because it not only discloses personality factors, but also attitudes. Attitude will often determine effectiveness more than skills will. This is something that cannot be taught, and many people are unaware that their problems in relationship to a group may be largely attitudinal. Testing can often pinpoint such a problem immediately.

Some psychological tests disclose trait weaknesses and vocational interests. These help the individual and the trainer to know precisely what areas need to be worked on. One extremely helpful test has been developed by Craig and Charters,[2] who have devised a checklist for industrial executives; this can be adapted to most situations to give some indication of the respective merits or weaknesses of an individual. In World Vision we often use what is known as the Worthington-Hurst tests to help determine leadership strengths and weaknesses.

There is a strong presumption that any person of comparatively low intelligence is not the best kind of prospect to consider for leadership responsibility. This does not mean that such a person cannot compensate. He may show superior qualities in other respects and can thus be greatly used by a given organization. Sometimes such people are strong in perseverance and possess an even temperament, which are assets to any group.

Not only does the trainer of leaders benefit from such testing programs, but the individual himself gains much personal insight through self-appraisal. When deficiencies are consciously faced, the trainer or someone else should help the person take the necessary steps to correct the problems indicated.

PERSONALITY CULTIVATION

Training should include both testing and personality cultivation. One church I know of requires all its elders to take the Dale Carnegie course. The best leader will want to bring all aspects of his life to bear on his goal of influencing others. Leadership training could well include public-speaking courses to bolster self-confidence. Many competent leaders weaken their effectiveness because they speak haltingly and poorly before groups. This greatly decreases their persuasiveness, which is a "must" ingredient to move people toward action.

HELPING TO MAKE TRAINING EFFECTIVE

Ordway Tead in his very helpful book *The Art of Leadership*[3] examines the various methods of giving leadership training expression. He provides five methods of instruction that may be adapted one way or another.

1. Experience in a leadership situation under some supervision;
2. Progression from small to larger leadership situations;
3. Apprentice courses of practice and study;
4. Conference study of methods by groups of leaders;
5. Systematic personal conferences of trainer and leader.

Experience in a leadership situation is so valuable an opportunity for training that many organizations ought to adopt it as a standing policy. When a department head is out sick or on vacation, for example, an assistant ought to assume the work responsibility. A new teacher substituting, a young minister out "candidating," and countless other situations arise which afford excellent means to provide experience. There is no substitute for this kind of training.

Progressive advancement is either planned or happens in a routine manner as assistants and others move up because of transfers and retirements. Usually this is not well supervised: if the person is likable and reasonably popular, his chances of success are good. But this routine method does not guarantee really good leadership, because too much is left to chance. With structured training and evaluation, the prospects of continued strong leadership run much higher.

PROBATIONARY PLACEMENT

Apprentice instruction is a method that can easily grow out of the leadership advancement just described. This method is often used in large stores, banks, and industrial organizations; churches find this to be a splendid method of gaining new leaders through internships. This method usually entails some formal study of the organization's history and objectives. After the study there is a probationary placement for a set period. If the individual does well, he is advanced when an administrative opening appears.

The procedure requires careful supervision and continuous contacts with the person. Tead cites some of the difficulties that may be encountered.

> There must be careful initial selection of apprentices; there must be real chances, not too long deferred, for promotion to posts of responsibility; the candidates must be prevented from getting swelled heads; there must be no artificial effort to hold those trained in the organization if they have outgrown the opportunities it can offer; there must be great care exercised that the rest of the organization does not come to feel that these apprentices are special favorites of the management rather than potential leaders who are advancing in their own right.[4]

Conferences organized for specific discussions on immediate needs are another highly successful means of finding and training future leaders. No phase of leadership today is exempt from rapid advances in knowledge and techniques. This is certainly true of Christian organizations. Refresher courses or "in-service training" can be most effective.

Finally, when leadership training is under way, many personal interviews with those having high potential is vital. The trainer has to be in close contact with the trainee's actual conduct on the job. Impressions and guidance can then best be offered in a face-to-face meeting; such meetings should be planned as to time and content. The higher the position of leadership, the more crucial such meetings are. A dangerous element in growing organizations is that there will be no one willing to offer the criticism or insight necessary to help people become better leaders.

MEASURING DEVELOPMENT

Development is fundamental, and it has to be measured or quantified in some way. If potential leaders have not learned to use effectively the material being taught them, the training program must be revised. Several criteria can measure this factor, although admittedly it is not easy. Ordway Tead offers five suggestions which have possible application to certain kinds of leadership situations.

1. The volume of work done by the group of which he is leader. It may be possible to measure this in terms of volume or cost per unit of man hours.

2. The quality of work done by the group. Sometimes this can be done by inspection, sometimes by studies of attitudes of clients, (colleagues,) [*sic*] customers or the public.

3. The stability of membership in the group. If there is a marked tendency for people to enter the group and then quickly resign, that is a bad sign. Figures of "labor turnover" are used in many organizations to discover such a tendency. And figures of the number of individuals who have stayed with the group for a given number of years can further show how stable the group is.

4. The number of complaints or grievances that is brought to the responsible directors of the group.

5. The opinion of the members of the group as to their own state of mind in relation to dealings with the leaders.[5]

In the final analysis, development of skills for leadership is judged successful by the performance. This lies not only in what a leader gets done, but in the satisfaction rendered, the sustained enthusiasm and effort put forth by the followers, and the depth of loyalty and attitudes manifested by the subordinates.

Notes

[1]J. Kenneth Wishart, *Techniques of Leadership* (New York: Vantage Press, 1965), p. 66.

[2]W. W. Charters, "The Discovery of Executive Talent" in *Handbook of Business Administration,"* ed. W. J. Donald, pp. 1604-1613.

[3]Ordway Tead, *The Art of Leadership* (New York: McGraw-Hill Book Co., Inc., 1963), pp. 289-99.

[4]Ibid., p. 293.

[5]Ibid., pp. 297-98.

CHAPTER THIRTEEN

Motivation and Leadership

A leader's success as a motivator is directly related to his sincerity in showing concern for his subordinates.

A leader often uses one particular style, perhaps without even realizing it, because of the way he views people and their motivations. Since the function of leadership is to lead, getting people to follow is of primary importance. For example, the bureaucratic leader somehow believes that everyone can agree on the best way to do things and that there is some system outside human relationships that can be the guide. Hence rules and regulations.

Individuals differ, not only in their ability to do and act, but also in their "will to do," or motivation. Motives are sometimes defined as needs, wants, drives, or impulses within the individual. Motives are directed toward goals, conscious or subconscious. Proper motivations are essential for strong and effective leadership.

The paternal leader wants everyone (including himself) to feel good. He believes that stress or tension within the group is bad for the organization (and perhaps even unchristian).

The laissez-faire leader usually makes one of two assumptions: either that the organization is running so well that he can't add anything to it, or that the organization really doesn't need a focal point of leadership.

The democratic leader who believes in participation usually enjoys solving problems and working with others. He assumes that others enjoy this same relationship. And he concludes that more is accomplished this way. This, he feels, is the best way to keep motivation high to attain goals.

The autocratic leader assumes that people do only what they are told, like regimented sheep. He alone knows what is best for all. This curbs motivation even though he may be a benevolent dictator.

To Motivate or Not

The "how-to" area of motivating employees or people is important, and sometimes we profit when we realize what not to do. M. M. Feinberg, quoted in *Managing Your Time,* gives an apt summary of how to motivate people. This industrial psychologist and personnel consultant says,

1. Never belittle a subordinate. (Destroys sense of self-worth and initiative.)

2. Never criticize a subordinate in front of others. (This temptation appears under pressure. Destroys rapport.)

3. Never fail to give subordinates your undivided attention. (Personal, undivided attention from time to time is imperative. Self-respect disappears with the realization that the boss will never give his undivided attention.)

4. Never seem preoccupied with your own interests. (Gives impression of selfishness and of manipulation of others for your own purposes.)

5. Never play favorites. (Quickly destroys morale of group.)

6. Never fail to help your subordinates grow. (The feeling that the boss is one who fights for his men is a great motivator. Inform them of openings, opportunities, and never hold them back out of self-interest.)

7. Never be insensitive to small things. (What may seem insignificant to you may be extremely important from the employees' perspective.)

8. Never embarrass weak employees. (While toleration of weakness in a key position often destroys the initiative of strong people, the manager must take care never to deal with this problem through causing embarrassment.)

9. Never vacillate in making a decision. (Indecision at the top breeds lack of confidence and hesitancy throughout an organization. Add this to other problems above and motivation may be irreparably damaged.)[1]

All consultants hold to the view that a leader's success as a motivator is directly related to his sincerity in showing concern for his subordinates. "The best way to motivate a subordinate," according to Feinberg, "is to show him that you are conscious of his needs, his ambitions, his fears and himself as an individual. The insensitive manager, who is perhaps unintentionally aloof, cold, impersonal and uninterested in his staff, usually finds it very difficult to get his people to put out an extra effort."[2] Feinberg's seventeen ways for a manager to show his concern and sensitivity for (hence to motivate) employees is helpful:

1. Communicate standards, and be consistent. (Minimizes mid-directed effort and motivates through known goals.)

2. Be aware of your own biases and prejudices. (Emotional reactions often color what should be objective judgment.)

3. Let people know where they stand. (Do this consistently through performance review or other methods. To withhold this critical information does the ultimate disservice to your organization — through demotivating the employee — and to the employee, who needs and has a right to know.)

4. Give praise when it is appropriate. (Properly handled, this is one of the most powerful motivators — especially in difficult performance areas or areas of anxiety.)

5. Keep your employees informed of changes that may affect them. (This doesn't mean telling them all company secrets, but you evidence your concern for them by informing them of matters in which they are likely to have a direct interest.)

6. Care about your employees. (Not only be attuned to the individual needs of those under you, but communicate this awareness.)

7. Perceive people as ends, not means. (To avoid the charge of using people for your own selfish goals, remember Thomas Cook, the explorer. He named a newly discovered island after the first man who spotted it. He regarded each man on the crew as a partner in the adventure and they loved him for the feeling of usefulness he gave them as individuals.)

8. Go out of your way to help subordinates. (A little extra effort, some personal inconvenience, goes a long way with subordinates in confirming the feeling that what they are doing is important to you . . . and that they are, too. Be sure the help you are giving is what is needed. Remember that in correcting an error, improving a deficiency, or strengthening a weakness, you must first know the individual. This may take hours of hard thought and experience.)

9. Take responsibility for your employees. (A part of caring is the willingness to assume some responsibility for what happens to

your employees. Be involved in their personal failures as well as their successes. A part of you fails or succeeds with them. As Frank Stanton, CBS president, asks his key people, "Is this the best job you and I can do together?" He thus demonstrates that he assumes partial responsibility and that he really cares.)

10. Build independence. (A supervisor who cares seeks to loosen and gradually drop the reins of supervision. Encourage independent thinking, initiative, resourcefulness.)

11. Exhibit personal diligence. (The most highly motivated leaders have the most highly motivated followers. Example is one of the best motivating factors.)

12. Be tactful with your employees. (Consideration, courtesy, sense of balance, appreciation and sensitivity to the views of others — all are important in dealing with employees.)

13. Be willing to learn from others. (Give new ideas a friendly reception, even when you know they will not work. This will encourage more creative thinking, and future ideas that may work.)

14. Demonstrate confidence. (Review any doubts you may have about your department, your staff, your projects or your company alone and in private. Demonstration of the leader's confidence builds confidence in his followers. Show by your behavior and speech that you are confident the work can be done; confident of your own responsibility; confident of their ability to handle the job.)

15. Allow freedom of expression. (Assuming your subordinates are reasonably competent, relax your vigil and allow them freedom to do things their way occasionally. Be more concerned with ultimate results than with methods of accomplishing them. This makes assignments much more interesting and challenging for subordinates.)

16. Delegate, delegate, delegate. (Assuming your people are competent and ambitious, delegate to them as much of your burden as you can. Recognize that pressure motivates and that most of us are not challenged to perform close to our capacity. Then, as much as possible, let them ride with their own decisions, learn from their own mistakes, and revel in their own successes.)

17. Encourage ingenuity. (The lowest-paid clerk may be ingenious. Challenge creativity by urging subordinates to beat your system of doing things. If your filing system isn't satisfactory, don't change it yourself; have your clerks and office manager tackle the job. The challenge to improve on the boss's system may bring surprising results.)[3]

One of the best means of motivating people is to let them participate in decision making. Such participation requires provision for systematic consultation in matters directly related to their tasks. Suggestions, recommendations, and advice are powerful stimulators and provide much motivational impact in any organization that has the courage to allow them.

WHAT ABOUT CHRISTIAN MOTIVATION?

There appears to be a tendency in Christian organizations to assume that motivation must never be examined, since this would border on a violation of the admonition not to judge. Not only is this admonition wholly applicable to management of Christian organizations, but the failure to make any effort to understand or utilize basic human motivation principles may be depriving our organizations of a principle source of energy, enthusiasm, creativity, and resourcefulness. This is not to gainsay the importance of dedication to the Lord's work: nothing can replace this ingredient.

How does one get people to do what has to be done? This question, which has been asked since people first worked together toward a common goal, has yet to be answered definitively. Social scientists in the management field have focused much attention on it recently. Sensitivity training is designed to make one more aware of the feelings of others. This is surely basic to understanding how to motivate, how to inspire, how to infuse a spirit of willingness to perform effectively.

For years the most effective motivation in industry was assumed to be the use of arbitrary authority and the threat of its use to withhold benefits or to impose penalties. Time and motion studies became the vogue for maximizing efficiency. Then came the realization that machinery and processes would run no better than people *wanted* them to. Slowdowns, strikes, and apathy could not be controlled with time and motion studies. The famous studies at the Hawthorne Works of Western Electric Company showed that simply putting a worker in a test situation provided sufficient interest and stimulation to ensure increased productivity even in the face of increasingly disadvantageous working conditions. Understanding what gives his people a feeling of recognition and importance is of primary importance to the manager. People who sense in their leader the ability to help them satisfy their needs will follow him willingly and enthusiastically.

Lack of unanimity in preferred leadership styles reflects, to some degree, difference of opinion over concepts of human relations. The manager who is primarily task-oriented will not consider human relations as important a factor in performance as the people-oriented

manager. Motivation is affected by such factors as degree of identification between organizational and personal goals, security, sense
of fulfillment and accomplishment, relations with associates and
superior, and income needs.

Among the most important principles of human behavior of
interest to managers are —

1. Behavior depends on *both* the person and his environment.
2. Each individual behaves in ways which *make sense to him.*
3. An individual's *perception of a situation* influences his behavior in
   that situation.
4. An individual's *view of himself influences what he does.*
5. An individual's behavior is influenced by his *needs,* which vary
   from person to person and from time to time.

A person's behavior may be changed in any one of three ways: by
changing his knowledge and skills; by helping the person change the
situation in which he works through modification of procedures or
assignments; or a combination of these.

Previous experience is known to be a primary factor in our
perception of a situation. Since one's experience is unique, highly
individualistic points of view inevitably result. For the leader this
underscores the importance of listening and observing to increase the
likelihood of behavioral change. Objective analysis and sympathetic
understanding of differing views may be the manager's most effective
tool in bringing about improved employee performance.

Psychologists say it is impossible to be completely objective
about what we do. We cannot, they say, remove our inner concerns
and self-concept from our actions. We can be more objective by
attempting to understand how our actions reflect our own concerns
and by taking this into account in our relationships with others.
Perhaps more importantly, we should realize that others also will
behave in ways that protect and enhance their inner feelings.

A very helpful passage appears in Kenneth Gangel's book *Competent to Lead,* in a chapter devoted to a Christian analysis of
motivation. Gangel says studies show that people do not necessarily
work better or sustain higher levels of loyalty to the group just
because they receive more benefits or more money. Because motivation is a psychological phenomenon, it is important to recognize what
psychologists have to say. Gangel quotes Mungo Miller, president of
Affiliated Psychological Services, who suggests the general principles psychologists have studied in their research on motivation.

1. Motivation is psychological, not logical. It is primarily an emotional process.

2. Motivation is fundamentally an unconscious process. The behavior we see in ourselves and others may appear to be illogical, but somehow, inside the individual, what he is doing makes sense to him.

3. Motivation is an individual matter. The key to a person's behavior lies within himself.

4. Not only do motivating needs differ from person to person, but in any individual they vary from time to time.

5. Motivation is inevitably a social process. We must depend on others for satisfaction of many of our needs.

6. In the vast majority of our daily actions, we are guarded by habits established by motivational processes that were active many years earlier.[4]

Gangel cites an address by Milton Rokeach, a professor of psychology at Michigan State University, on the subject of how people change. Rokeach said there are five different kinds of beliefs that can help Christian leaders develop Christian value systems in children, youth, and adults. All these beliefs are not equally important to the individual. Therefore, Rokeach declared, the more important a belief, the more it will resist change; the more trivial the belief, the easier it is to change. He concluded that the more important the belief that is changed, the greater the effects of it.

First for Rokeach are primitive beliefs that are fundamental. They are the ones that would have 100 percent social acceptability. Therefore they would have the greatest resistance to change.

Second are the beliefs that involve a deep personal experience. They do not depend upon social support, but are based on experience and not whether anyone else accepts them. The more realistic the experience, the more unshakable the belief. Obviously these beliefs are not always consistent with reality; to induce change, a person must be helped to see his fantasy system.

Third, there are authority beliefs. We develop beliefs about authorities whom we can trust and those we cannot. Again, these concepts may be contrary to reality, but the leader must be aware of them because they are held tenaciously.

Fourth are peripheral beliefs. Rokeach explained that this kind of belief is like an authority belief because it is a derivation. Rather than focusing on the authority, the belief is in something the authority has said. Such a belief he calls peripheral because this belief can easily be changed if the authority changes.

Fifth, inconsequential beliefs are the least important to an organization because it matters little whether a person believes a Ford or a Chevy is a better car.

Understanding these beliefs is helpful to Christian leaders and organizations because so many Christians hold beliefs that are fuzzy and confused. They often are not sure what is truly authoritative and what is inconsequential. If they lose faith in the authority, then they lose faith in the church, a Christian value system, and so on. They feel let down, and this affects their motivation. It is good to realize that peripheral beliefs are extremely weak because the authority figure can easily shift, as from pastor to university professor.

THE WILL HAS TO BE CHANGED

We've all heard about the strange illness that afflicts many churchgoers, called "Sabbaticus." It seems that right after breakfast such people get a strange paralysis so that they are unable to go to church. Then about noon it disappears. That afternoon they feel great at the baseball game or picnic in the park. None of us can be too critical of this behavior, because in the final analysis each of us has similar weaknesses of will on one matter or another.

But to increase motivation, a leader is required to stimulate people to a feeling of dissatisfaction with the status quo. Because dissatisfaction creates an inner tension, the person must act to restore the imbalance to normal. Thus the leader has to touch the will in order to help the person and provide the proper steps for him to move from point A to point B.

The leader has to show the person how to apply himself to take the necessary actions to reach the objective. A major stimulant is to arouse in the subordinates the feelings that success can be assured and that the task is important and carries a measure of status. Esprit de corps must be instilled.

A word of caution must be sounded: it is neither good nor right to ask a person to undertake a task for which he has absolutely no ability. This surely destroys motivation. The Peter Principle (which simply indicates that a person can be promoted beyond his abilities to a "level of incompetence") is always lurking; a good leader is attuned to know what happens in the personality structure of people whose mental equipment makes it impossible for them to function at higher levels. Furthermore, he should be aware of what such errors in judgment can mean to an organization. Autos and airplanes should not be driven to go beyond the speed the designer has planned; under too much stress, something will give way. The same applies to human beings.

Notes

[1]Quoted from *Effective Psychology for Managers* by M. M. Feinberg (Englewood Cliffs, N.J.: Prentice-Hall, Inc., 1965).
[2]Ibid.
[3]Ibid.
[4]Kenneth O. Gangel, *Competent to Lead* (Chicago: Moody Press, 1974), p. 85.

CHAPTER FOURTEEN

The Major Tasks of Leaders

The task-oriented leader always places the desire for achievement and joy of accomplishment above status, power, or money.

Most authors historically have agreed that the managerial functions of planning, organizing, motivating, and controlling are considered central to any discussion of management and leadership.

These functions are basic and relevant, regardless of the kind of organization we lead or level of management with which we are concerned.

Acting in our managerial capacity, all of us — presidents, department heads, foremen, supervisors, pastors, executives — do basically the same thing. We are each and all engaged in part in getting things done with and through people. Each of us must, at one time or another, carry out all the duties characteristic of managers. Even a well-run household uses these managerial functions, though in many cases they are used intuitively.

Today's effective leader gets things done because he utilizes a workable style and has the ability to motivate others highly. He also becomes successful when he is task-oriented. This means he must learn the resources available to his organization and study the means to arrive at goals. He must have the ability to define policies and procedures to organize the activities of his people toward the common goal.

As indicated, a popular definition of leadership is that it is the art or science of getting things done through people. This becomes a reality through the four principal managerial tasks. This chapter deals with what I consider to be the two fundamental tasks — planning, and then organizing these plans into a suitable framework.

Planning involves setting goals and objectives for the organization and developing "work maps" showing how these goals and objectives are to be accomplished. Once plans have been laid, organizing becomes meaningful. This involves bringing together resources — people, capital, and equipment — in the most effective way to accomplish the goals. Organizing and planning, therefore, involves an integration of resources.

It is generally agreed that there are at least three kinds of skill necessary for carrying out the process of management: technical, human, and conceptual.

> *Technical skill* — Ability to use knowledge, methods, techniques, and equipment necessary for the performance of specific tasks acquired from experience, education, and training.
>
> *Human skill* — Ability and judgment in working with and through people, including an understanding of motivation and an application of effective leadership.
>
> *Conceptual skill* — Ability to understand the complexities of the overall organization and where one's own operation fits in. This knowledge permits one to act according to the objectives of the total organization rather than only on the basis of the goals and needs of one's own immediate group.

Planning, in capsule form, is spelling out goals, defining them. This includes long-range, intermediate, and short-range. These goals must be reachable within a certain time frame. And it is always wise to have an alternate plan. It is said that as a military strategist Napoleon was without peer because he always was ready with an immediate second plan in case the first one didn't work.

PLANNING STARTS WITH GOALS

Goal-setting is the starting point for results. It may go by a number of names in the business world such as "management by objectives," "performance standards," or "management for results." For our purposes, I prefer to make a distinction between the setting of goals and their achievement.

Without goal-setting, the process of hoped-for achievement becomes a rudderless operation and wastes time. It is true that one hour at the drafting board in the mechanical engineering field can literally save many hours in the shop. This illustrates what I mean, because execution demands extensive thought on how best to accomplish the task.

Goal-setting must be specific. Vague, general goals may have a place early in the game, but eventually we must have specifics in mind. "We want to produce a quality product" and "let's sell as much as possible" are goals much too broad to bring any real results. A football team has the long-range goal to carry the ball into the opponent's end zone, but it must be committed to the more immediate, specific goals of how to arrive there yard by yard.

Objectives must be not only specific, but attainable and measurable. For example, it would be foolish for a firm, without increasing its sales force or advertising, to net a profit of say $2 million one year and then expect a jump to $5 million the next.

Goal-setting is extremely important for nonprofit and Christian organizations as well. This is not always so easy, because their goals have often not been clearly defined. A church, for example, cannot realistically set a goal for gaining new members unless it knows the course taken to bring it where it is presently.

Specific Objectives

To help you begin to set goals, this outline is suggested:

> *Instructions:* In developing your objectives (usually not more than five at any one time) cover each of the following areas if appropriate. It is often useful to indicate, as an example, that no additional equipment is needed or that no outside assistance will be required.

I. State the objective briefly.

II. Restate the objective in quantitative terms. (You can usually improve on your first statement of this objective. If this is done, skip item I in submitting your statement of objective to your superior.)

III. Reason for (or effect of) achieving this objective.

IV. Outline plan to achieve objective.

V. Timing.

    A. Date for completion

    B. Date for starting

    C. Planned check points (dates and status of work) — review of work, progress, etc.

VI. Assistance needed to achieve objective.

    A. Resources under your control (If not likely to be available when needed, how will they be obtained?)

    1. Amount of your time to be required

    2. Subordinates who will be involved (by name or by qualifications required and amount of time required)

    3. Materials and supplies to be used (list)

    4. Equipment and space to be used (list)

    5. Other expenses required (list, but exclude items to be listed under VI-B and VI-C)

    6. Supervision needed — by whom and from whom

  B. Assistance needed from others in the organization (specify what, when, from whom, and amount)

  C. From outside sources (specify what, when, from whom, and amount or cost)

VII. Total cost to achieve objective should not exceed $_____.

VIII. If objective is not undertaken, the cost may be $_____. Explanation:

  IX. How results will be measured. (If you have difficulty determining how results will be measured, review item II — you may not have restated the objective as clearly as possible.)

   X. To meet planned schedule, approval should be received by

    _____.

  XI. Guides for selecting specific objectives.

    A. Is it within the duties and responsibilities of the position? (The position description can be revised!)

    B. Does it have a favorable impact on the present and future success of the enterprise as a whole? (Not just a unit of the organization unless it contributes to the overall objective.)

    C. Can it be accomplished within a reasonable time, e.g., six to twelve months? (Longer objectives can have intermediate goals established.)

    D. Is it to be achieved by the incumbent in addition to standard performance of regular duties and responsibilities? (Again, the position description can be revised.)

    E. One objective should be to assist others to meet their objectives.

Twins: Achievement and Goals

Every study of the successful executive places the desire for achievement, the joy of accomplishment, ahead of just about everything else — money, power, or status.

Most important, we find that the drive for achievement and joy of accomplishment are tied to and associated with a striving for new and original solutions to problems.

Therefore, *leadership begins with the desire to achieve, the desire to raise the standard, the desire to attain goals.*

> To achieve, the leader must set goals
> To set goals, he must make decisions
> To reach goals, he must plan
> To plan, he must analyze
> To analyze, he must implement
> To implement, he must organize
> To organize, he must delegate
> To delegate, he must administrate
> To administrate, he must communicate
> To communicate, he must motivate
> To motivate, he must share
> To share, he must care
> To care, he must believe
> To believe, he must set goals that inspire
>   belief and the desire to achieve
> Thus, the "process of leadership" begins
>   and ends with goals!

Some of the following material on planning is adapted from our World Vision International "Christian Leadership Letter" (May-June, 1973).

PLANNING IS TRYING TO WRITE FUTURE HISTORY

Man is a future-oriented being. He plans on the basis of what he has perceived in the past, but he tries to project this understanding into the future. Except for the most simple, close-in projects, it is very unlikely that our predictions about the future will be 100 percent accurate. The adage "If something can go wrong, it probably will" is another way of saying that there are so many possibilities that something other than what we expected and hoped for will happen, that the probability of things happening *our* way is remote.

Planning is an attempt to move from "Now" to "Then," to change things from "The Way Things Are" to "The Way Things Ought to Be."

Since no man can be sure of the future, why plan? Basically to improve the probability that what we believe should happen will happen. The point of the planning arrow figuratively touches the goal. The steps that need to be accomplished stretch back along the arrow into the present to create a "plan."

Planning Is a Process

If plans are considered fixed and unchangeable, they most likely will fail. Planning is a process. The necessary steps are laid out, pointing toward the future goal, but as each major step is taken, a reevaluation must take place. Between the time the plans are conceived and the first step is taken, *change* occurs. An unforeseen obstacle may appear. A more appropriate method may be uncovered. The goal may have shifted.

This is why into all our planning there needs to be designed a reevaluation or feedback process that first calls us to reexamine the future at each step and then measures the extent of our program. If we have set a goal to have one hundred new members in our church during the next twelve months, we had better not wait until the eleventh month to see how we are doing. If we are planning to drive a thousand miles across unfamiliar territory, it is best to look at the road map once in a while and measure progress. If we plan to train a group for a new assignment and put them to work in six months, periodic checkpoints will be needed.

Yet time and time again we fail to evaluate progress. Sometimes we even set up an evaluation program and then fail to use it. Why? Many times it's because the measurement may take as much energy as the program itself. At other times we are so engrossed in our task that we just forget (or don't want) to ask, "How are we doing?"

Planning Takes Time

Evaluation is worth every minute. But most of us won't do it unless we consciously set time aside. A daily time to make up a things-to-do list should be a habit. Setting times of monthly, quarterly, and yearly review on our calendars will build the process into the regular "work" we need to do each day.

Because planning takes time, it should begin as far in advance as possible. In a church, don't wait until October to start planning for the next year. The process should begin no later than April or May, so that as many people as possible can be brought in and you are not rushed into the future.

Evaluation should, therefore, be just as much a part of planning as the steps toward the goal. *Someone* should be made responsible for the measurement, usually not the person responsible for the achievement.

Planning Is Both Personal and Corporate

Don't be misled into believing that planning for tomorrow is useful only for groups. Goal-setting and planning must become a personal style of life if they are to be truly effective. There is a direct relationship between a man's effectiveness in his personal life and his effectiveness in his organizational life.

Once all the alternative approaches have been analyzed and put aside and final plans have been laid, it is useful to remember that each step of the plan is actually a goal in itself. Each step should therefore have the same characteristics as the end goal of the project: it should be accomplishable and measurable. It should also have a deadline and the name of the person responsible. Regardless of what method of planning is used (and there are many), failure to assign dates and responsible individuals to each step will lessen the probability of success.

Sometimes, once a goal has been set, the steps needed to reach that goal — plans — are immediately apparent. But often we need to gather as many ideas as possible before going further. If these suggestions can come forth from the group that is going to carry on the work, so much the better.

PLANNING TO FAIL

There are various reasons why executives fail to plan, but they probably can be reduced to two major ones. The first is that planning rarely falls into the category of emergency and therefore does not appear to be urgent. Therefore one can easily become the prey of procrastination.

The second reason is that leaders usually consider themselves people of action. Planning, for many of them, is too slow a process, and they become impatient with details. They want to get on with the job without giving enough time and study to analyzing the best way to accomplish it.

This will not happen if leaders set a goal for themselves to set goals. When they reserve a regular time for this, the discipline will produce results. A few minutes for goal-setting and planning *every* day in the morning or at the close of the working hours will be highly effective. The more one systematically plans, the easier it will become.

Most organizations fail to plan sufficiently, but they may also have the opposite problem. Certain individuals may plan a great deal, but fail to take action. The following is a checklist to help build self-confidence in the planning process by deciding who is going to do what and when:

1. Recognize goal-seeking as the most important activity of leadership.
2. Recognize that, although important, it is never urgent.

3. Set aside specific times for planning activities.

4. Establish specific, measurable goals in all areas of activity.

5. Involve others in planning in a creative way.

6. Establish a creative climate that is tolerant of occasional errors.

7. Train all levels of supervision in planning and see that they do it.

8. Bring in an outside consultant or consultants who understand goal-seeking and can act as a catalyst.

9. Learn from the experience of others through studying management literature.

10. Create reminder cards and signs, and post them in prominent places.

11. Recognize goal-seeking as a universal technique, and apply it in all areas of activity.

12. Establish control-feedback and a system for constant evaluation of plans and objectives.

13. Place the emphasis on goals rather than methods to achieve them.

14. Always consider cost effectiveness.

15. Establish both long- and short-range goals.

16. See that short-range goals are coordinated with long-range goals.[1]

CHRISTIANS NEED HELP

Because true leadership is an act, it requires planning. I have found that a major weakness in many of our evangelical Christian enterprises is in planning — long-range planning, over a three-to-five-year span. Christians are not generally accustomed to thinking this far ahead, for most have heard from Sunday school days that Jesus may return at any moment. Such truth forever remains, but it should never inhibit growth by short-circuiting responsible planning for the future.

Long-range planning is what one well-known author on management calls "risk-taking decision making." Such planning takes courage because of the risk factor. Such risk-taking action is sometimes misunderstood. It is not —

—Forecasting. Forecasting attempts to find the most probable course.

—Concerned with future decisions. It is concerned rather with the future of *present* decision.

—An attempt to eliminate risk. (It means the capacity to take greater risks — and the right risks.) "It is never safe to play it safe."

An outstanding story of World War II that discloses the importance of planning is the British offensive against the German Army in North Africa. Under General Erwin Rommel, the Germans had pushed nearly the whole way to Cairo. In desperation, the British High Command assigned the task of turning the situation around to Field Marshall Bernard Montgomery.

Immediately Montgomery let it be known that he was going to take the initiative. He planned carefully with great detail. Throughout the whole chain of command down to the privates, each person was told specifically what his job was to be. A perfectly coordinated team was formed, and each man knew precisely the commander's objectives and how they were to be achieved. When the British offensive began with this great precision, the mighty German army was routed, and it became one of the early turning points of that war.

Montgomery was successful because through solid planning he was able to excite, motivate, and challenge all his troops. The challenge to them to perform made the difference.

Planning spells the difference. Remember that it is work done today to cause to happen tomorrow what we specifically want to happen.

THE NEXT STEP

Whereas planning has more to do with *ideas,* organizing has to do with *things.* Specific tools such as time, materials, schedule, training, and man-hours are to be utilized. Organizing is needed to carry out the plan, because it will be done through people. As I see it, organizing is the second major task of responsible leadership because, of necessity, it follows planning.

Organizing has to begin with the job description of the leader. With this he is prepared to assemble the needed resources and be better equipped to determine who is going to do what.

An increasingly popular means for better organizing or for strengthening an organization is the use of a coordinated team approach in which problem-solving teams at each level in the organization meet at prescribed intervals. Representatives then communicate among the departments and on that basis make the daily decisions required. This provides a continuous coordination through the whole organization, allows group creativity, reduces interdepartmental conflicts, facilitates decision-making, and permits personnel a greater participation in company policy. This develops positive attitudes. Such an approach is a powerful means to help an organization sustain its momentum and reach its goals faster and better.

ORGANIZATION CRITICS

In our sophisticated Western society, however, the trend in recent years has been toward decentralization and less organization. In academic circles, for instance, it has been taught that too much structure inhibits flexibility. This means, of course, that growth and creativity cannot easily be fostered.

But it can be clearly seen that numerous organizations lie buried in oblivion because they failed to structure enough. Without establishing the proper lines of authority and delegation, they foundered, unable to use and maximize the potential within their group. In an earlier chapter, we saw how Moses' father-in-law, Jethro, gave advice much like a management consultant: "Moses, you can't do the job all by yourself — you've got to organize!"

There are many critics of organizational flow charts today, yet such charts are genuinely needed. There is no advantage in throwing out the baby with the bath water. What is needed in many cases is not to discard charts, but to adjust them at regular intervals whenever and however the organization changes. This helps to guarantee a healthy organization that keeps plans timely.

Organizational planning is perhaps the major foundation for all planning, because it clarifies the formal lines of responsibility and authority. A flow chart should not limit worker creativity; the key to dynamic growth is permitting an increase in worker participation.

CLARIFY DISTINCTIONS

The functions within any group fall into two basic categories: line and staff functions. Authorities may disagree on their distinctions or use, but the main distinction is that staff personnel advise, and the line people actually perform.

The most vivid illustration of these functions is in the military. Frequently problems exist in this arrangement. But the best solution is for staff personnel to serve as assistants to line supervisors, or to procure outside consultants who will help in the training and guidance of personnel.

MAKING IT MEANINGFUL

Organizing, in the final analysis, is *arranging* and *relating* the work to be done so that it may be performed most effectively by people. This includes the following:

1. Delegating — entrusting responsibility and authority to others and creating accountability for results

2. Establishing and maintaining interpersonal human relationships

3. Preparation of position descriptions — a written statement of end results expected, activities, organizational relationships, and ac-

countability detailing a person and his job within the organization

4. Job standards — criteria by which results will be evaluated

5. Performance appraisal — a face-to-face appraisal of work in progress and end results

Remember that the function of organizing management or leadership is —

1. To develop organizational structure

2. To delegate responsibility

3. To establish relationships

TRAINING IS VITAL

Prepare an organization chart and constantly revise it. Recognize, however, that this is only a start. Training is a vital part of organizing. Training is teaching a person to do something; it is not orientation. A training program should enable people, upon completion of the program, to do some things that they were unable to do previously.

Every good leader knows that training leads to competence, and without it no organization can flourish. The investment of time and money pay rich dividends, for no one is immune from learning more about his work, responsibilities, and abilities. Even a highly trained secretary must continue to develop skills, because new machines and methods are continually producing change in an office. Training, therefore, is not only for the orientation of new staff people, but to produce better performance by those already on the job.

Volumes can be written on this subject. Perhaps the best resource to develop a training program is the American Management Association, which can supply information needed for the best possible training in a specific organization.

Small organizations usually have difficulty in training, because their leaders feel their budgets are unable to include this "luxury." How wrong and hurtful to growth this attitude is.

Knowledge of what constitutes excellent leadership is needed for starting a successful training program. Executives or organizational officers must be convinced that it is vital to success. It is so important that leaders should not delegate training to lower levels and then ignore it.

COMMITMENT TO THE GROUP

We deal with the subject of commitment more fully in the chapters that concern motivation and leadership excellence. But we must reinforce the fact that every successful leader has to be committed to the task of meeting the needs of the group at the working level.

He must always stand ready to help furnish definitions to help to clarify the group's tasks and objectives. To do this, he must be ready to assign specific tasks, request information, and submit needed data.

Statistically we know now that in this country more people leave their jobs because of some personal problem with the group leader or fellow employees than because of some incompetence in their work leading to their firing. People lose their desire to work on a team if they are unhappy. Thus every leader must always be aware that group dynamics is the driving spiritual, moral, or intellectual force of a specific group. Each group has its own dynamic, so the leader must be in touch on a deep level to be effective in strengthening interpersonal relationships.

At stake is mainly loyalty — loyalty to the group's leaders and loyalty to one another. The perceptive leader will sense the group's feelings or moods, and he will aggressively try to heal breaches, reduce tension, and keep the communication channels open.

Effective leadership is not only a matter of using good tools and practices to attain tasks designed for others. It must begin with a leader's own established plans and goals, which then need to be placed into proper priorities, programs, and schedules.

Fulfilling the tasks outlined in this chapter will build your organization. It will attract and nurture good leadership. It will help all involved to set high standards of conduct, responsibility, and performance. This in turn will provide greater motivation, pride in work, and a more fulfilled life, with each one knowing that he is contributing significantly to his generation.

Notes

[1]Frank Goble, "Excellence in Leadership" (New York: American Management Association, 1972), p. 18.

CHAPTER FIFTEEN

The Leader Implements the Plan

Proper direction will always determine whether the production of goods and services will meet quality standards and be available at the right time and place as well as at a reasonable cost.

In an excellent paper entitled "The Institution as Servant," Robert Greenleaf writes:

The traditional view of organization sees the modus operandi of any institution in three parts, with one overarching element.

1. *Goals* and *Strategy*, including long-range thinking that culminates in plans.

2. *Organization,* the concern with people and structure, the reasonably durable arrangements, and the staffing for carrying out plans.

3. *Implementation,* the day-to-day execution of plans, including administrative initiative and response to situations. It is the use made of organization to carry out the plans.

Overarching these three is the exercise of *leadership* which gives the total process coherent and dynamic force by establishing priorities, allocating resources, choosing and guiding staff, articulating goals and philosophy, and exerting a sustained goal for excellence.

Planning and organizing are essential, but alone are insufficient for obtaining the desired results in management or leadership. The problems of coordinating and controlling to implement and strengthen the plans must also be solved. To accomplish this, a leader will be assisted in great measure through other means.

The purpose of this chapter is to suggest other tasks by which leaders may at least begin to direct or coordinate their activities with others.

The first point for discussion is the relationship of coordination and control to management. Before members of any group can coordinate their activities, the leader must complete these four steps: (1) he and they must know or define the common goals of the whole group, as discussed in chapter 14; (2) the specific areas of responsibility for each of the individuals must be spelled out; (3) standards of performance must be identified so each person will know what will be considered a good job; these standards may be set in terms of cost, quantity, quality, service, time, or other measurable criteria; and (4) the results of each man's work must be measured.

To attain the common goals, a leader must provide direction that follows the major tasks of planning and organizing. This involves several important functions: (1) staffing, or the selection of people, (2) genuine communication, (3) delegation, and (4) decision-making. Let us look at them in this order.

STAFFING

Most organizations, including Christian ones, doubtless overlook the importance of this leadership task. Often more attention is given to the selection and purchase of new equipment: months may go by and numerous bids studied before a decision is made on some great new piece of machinery, but the vital task of staffing is frequently not given adequate attention. I believe without question the greatest financial losses to all kinds of organizations lie in mistakes made in people selection. Comparative costs have been revealed by industry, for example, and the losses are staggering.

It is impossible to treat this subject exhaustively in this book. But I want to stress several key points here. One must always remember that many factors go into making decisions about placement. Not only are qualifications for a specific job important, but other placement criteria need to be examined thoroughly, such as skill, promotion, opportunities, interests, the kind of supervision a person needs or wants, and the kind of fellow workers the applicant finds the most congenial. And do not forget the importance of selecting people with the greatest potential for growth in your organization.

Another important guideline is the observation that while rank-and-file employees can do well in the lower and middle-management levels, they seldom are able to find their niche in top management.

Rarely can this kind of person be useful that high because the now-famous Peter Principle takes hold. The reason for this is that those qualities necessary for successful top managers — breadth of perspective, genuine self-confidence, self-reliance, and compulsive drive — are usually missing in those people who have leveled off at a particular position.

I cannot stress too strongly that this task of staffing is crucial, because if the wrong people are hired, no organization can function properly. There is always a one-to-one correlation between the level of personnel and the quality of achievement attained by them. Many Christian organizations are often guilty of hiring mediocre personnel because highly competent, well-trained people are often in short supply.

When a leader-employer hires hastily, he will usually regret the decision. Many organizations have moved to the policy of hiring people for a probationary period — say 90 to 120 days. This weeds out incompetence and helps to save face for leaders who may need to release or relieve people of a given job. It also helps to give the new employees some incentive and provides security to know that after such a period they have a permanent position.

THINKING ABOUT SELECTION

The abundance of material written on this subject can be reduced to several important guidelines that must be followed for the best results.

The first prerequisite is time to think through the kind of person needed and to define what criteria to use to select him. Various screening methods may have to be used, as well as researching and studying the market so as to recognize the proper sources for potential personnel. If this latter process is prolonged, the best prospects may be lost. This leadership task should be given top priority.

It is true more often than not, unless a highly skilled person is required, that current employees can fill the vacancy through proper training. This should always be investigated before a search begins outside the organization. We do well to remember that when an organization does go outside in its search, current employees present an excellent source of leads for new people.

Many criteria have been devised to screen applicants for a position, but one of the most important is a thorough investigation of an applicant's performance on previous jobs. Seldom is this done thoroughly enough. Jack McQuaig of the McQuaig Institute of Executive Training has written a book, *How to Pick Men* (New York:

Frederick Fell, Inc., 1963), which is extremely perceptive and practical.

THERE'S MORE TO IT

Staffing does not end simply with the selection of personnel. The leader must also have a program of continuing evaluation of performance, appraising possible promotions and salary increases as merited.

For further study I highly recommend the book *The Selection Process: Choosing the Right Man for the Job* by Milton M. Mandell (New York: American Management Association, 1964).

After selection or staffing, a key task of the leader is to help people improve their knowledge, attitudes, and skills. Even when jobs are occupied by people who have the aptitudes and ability to perform, you should give attention to improvement. The development of concepts and new techniques in a given field increases with the development of people, and this alone is significant.

Hundreds of millions of dollars are spent each year in industry for management development and training programs. But still there appears to be a shortage of strong leadership potential. There may be two reasons for this. One is that promotion is emphasized far more than development; the other is that frequently development is not supported at top management levels. Without realizing it, leaders often doom the ultimate success of programs because they show too little active interest, though they may give token consent or encouragement to their key people.

After a while, middle management, knowing that top management is too busy to bother, loses interest in development. I believe that the most successful leaders place personnel development among their highest priorities.

Development requires a relaxing atmosphere for the trainee. The best kind of leadership is a creative process. We know that people use only a fraction of their creative potential; it is readily seen that creative people can more easily handle problems despite failure, because they have a high self-esteem that provides inner drive. Creativity does not come naturally for most of us. If a person really wants to develop this quality, he must increase the amount of time devoted to actual creative thinking.

Creative problem-solving may be approached in several ways, but all follow a formula:

1. Define the problem — decide what it is or what goal you want to achieve.

2. Assemble the known facts about the situation and list some of the possible solutions.

3. Decide what additional facts are necessary and work out a plan to assemble them.

4. With all available facts at hand, think intently about these facts and possible solutions.

5. Allow a period of incubation; that is, forget the problem for a while and turn your mind to other matters, but keep paper and pencil handy to jot down any ideas that may occur to you.

6. Re-examine the problem and reach a decision based on the ideas that have come to you during the period of incubation.[1]

Often leaders won't allow creativity in others because they lack the trait themselves. The greatest obstacles in the way of a leader's creativity usually lie within his own personality. If he manifests paranoidal suspicions of others, he will not allow himself to be challenged by their suggestions for growth or change. If he is critical or insecure within himself, he will be afraid to step out with new ideas for fear of rejection. New ideas challenge deeply entrenched ones. If a person is insecure he will be highly defensive, and this stymies growth or change.

DIRECTING REQUIRES COMMUNICATING

A second function necessary to enhance the leader's task of directing is effective communication.

"There's a lot of communication these days on the subject of communication," said a gentleman after attending a seminar on the subject. "The trouble is that the speaker just doesn't understand our situation."

The seminar leader, well known as the chairman of the department of communications at a state university, had failed to communicate. He knew all the proper language and theories. He projected facts, but not understanding.

This incident may be repeated scores of times in different ways. Communication is blocked when emotions do not coincide with another's feelings or when there is selective listening on the hearer's part. An appreciation of these factors will enable leaders to take better steps to guarantee effective communication in their own group.

The issue can be put another way. Do you communicate without trying, or do you try without communicating? Because people respond more to how we feel about them than what we say to them, it behooves every leader to assess the depth of acceptance he brings to his relationships in his organization.

DIRECTING REQUIRES INFLUENCING

If leadership is an act to get people to follow, then it goes without saying that a leader's task is to bring together human desire, skill, and energy so that the common goal will be achieved. To accomplish this, he must influence others by various kinds of communication. Ordway Tead suggests at least eight different methods: (1) suggestion, (2) imitation, (3) exhortation, (4) persuasive argument, (5) publicity, (6) reliance upon the logic of events, (7) a show of affectionate devotion, and (8) using problem situations which in themselves create pressures.[2]

Suggestions are usually verbal. The power of suggestion has been tested, and it can go far toward getting results in emotional appeals. The wise leader will occasionally use this medium.

Imitation is a reliable way to influence others. A leader's cause must be well established; when people see the real thing, they are far more apt to copy or follow along. This method heightens unity of purpose and direction.

Exhortation is perhaps the opposite of suggestion because it is direct whereas suggestion is more nondirective. Imparting information is needed, but exhortation has its limitations and should be used guardedly. The problem is to sustain high motivation over a long period of time, because exhortation is easily forgotten. Also, when constant repetition is used to get a point across, it may soon wear thin. Yet if wisely used, exhortation can bring powerful results.

Publicity is a technique that helps to build prestige and strength. It intends to influence others by facts and the disclosure of data so as to move people toward some concerted action. This is currently one of the most powerful media of influence, and a wise leader will cultivate it.

I believe that a real key to directing and holding organizations together is communication, both spoken and written. Seldom does it receive enough attention, but it is basic to human relationships.

More Than Talking

We have all heard people who talk a lot but really don't say anything. But there's another problem in communication. J. C. Penney used to say that one of the occupational diseases of a poor leader was the inability to listen. Listening to the whole story and assisting at the right time with a kind word can be crucial. Encouraging people in order to draw them out requires that a leader be in touch with people where they are.

But *real* communication is more than verbalization. The best definition I have read is offered by a friend of mine: "Real communication is feeling what the other person is feeling at the moment and accepting him for it." Having a deep feeling for subordinates is a true key to building bridges in human relations. Without it, detachment sets in, affecting quality work and attitudes.

Here are some suggestions to help you in communication:

1. Stop talking!
   You cannot listen if you are talking.
   Polonius (*Hamlet*): "Give every man thine ear, but few thy voice."

2. Put the talker at ease.
   Help him feel that he is free to talk.
   This is often called a "permissive environment."

3. Show him that you want to listen.
   Look and act interested. Do not read your mail while he talks.
   Listen to understand rather than to reply.

4. Remove distractions.
   Don't doodle, tap, or shuffle papers.
   Will it be quieter if you shut the door?

5. Empathize with him.
   Try to put yourself in his place so that you can see his point of view.

6. Be patient.
   Allow plenty of time. Do not interrupt him.
   Don't start for the door or walk away.

7. Hold your temper.
   An angry man gets the wrong meaning from words.

8. Go easy on argument and criticism.
   This puts him on the defensive. He may "clam up" or get angry.
   Do not argue: even if you win, you lose.

9. Ask questions.
   This encourages him and shows you are listening.
   It helps to develop points further.

10. Stop talking!
    This is first and last, because all other commandments depend on it. You just can't do a good listening job while you are talking.

Nature gave man two ears but only one tongue, which is a gentle hint that he should listen more than he talks. The major benefits of good listening are (1) A good listener can make better decisions because he has better information; (2) a good listener saves time because he learns more within a given period of time; (3) listening helps the communicator determine how well his message is being received; (4) a good listener stimulates others to better speaking; (5) good listening decreases misunderstanding.

How to Communicate

When good communication exists, it helps to create a solid form of understanding within the organization. This in turn heightens the persuasive element. People then are motivated to accomplish their assignments. When the lines of communication are open and all people within the organization are cognizant of them, feedback will be automatic. We need responses to test continually the goals and methods employed to bring results. This helps to elevate attitudes and provides the answer to the question that all employees have: "Why do we do it this way?"

1. Success in communication depends upon gaining acceptance of what is said. Therefore the communicator must carefully plan, not only what to tell, but how to tell it.

2. One of the best ways to gain acceptance is to give meaningful reasons to those being informed.

3. Where persuasion is needed, the oral word can be more effective than the printed word. A face-to-face discussion gives an opportunity to observe reaction and to adapt the presentation to gain the required end.

4. Keep the channels open both ways by inviting employee response. Communications will flow down more easily if a few observations and opinions flowing up are welcomed — even unpleasant ones.

5. In planning to communicate, always seek more than one method. A meeting which is reinforced by a letter sent home is more effective than an announcement made only one time.

6. Communication is not completed until the communicator is certain that his message was received and interpreted accurately. The receiver should consider, "What did he mean by that?" The transmitter, therefore, should consider, "What is he likely to think that I mean by this?"

Real communication filters out false reasoning and helps a leader to make better judgments. It also provides the means of finding where others are in their feelings, goals, and attitudes. This is so essential to a well-functioning organization. Communication skills can be acquired by most, and the effort to attain them will be reflected a thousandfold by those who take the time and spend the energy to develop this trait.

The effective leader learns to use communication in such a positive manner that it strengthens the unity of an organization, rather than dividing it. This means he has to keep the channels open — when there is a message that may bring disagreement or overt hostility — until the problem is completely resolved. This is not always easy, because it may threaten the leader unless he is mature and clearly understands the communication process.

A leader's task is to develop the positive side of human relations through the proper use of interpersonal communication. The starting point is to understand people's needs. If he does, the leader will not convey a cold image before others, and people find it easier to unburden themselves to him, which is vital to communicating effectively.

Communication is enhanced within an organization if it is structured for it. When managerial responsibility is broken up into smaller units, this encourages communication. A leader's spending time individually with all his departmental executives engenders rapport. Where people are encouraged to provide more input, they will tend to be less negative and contribute more through interaction.

CHANNELS OF COMMUNICATION

There can be little communication without channels to convey it. Formal channels include regularly scheduled meetings, information memos, creative use of a bulletin board, and the like. An informal channel is one that carries the message although the organization has not specifically planned for it. Lee Thayer talks about the communication channels with the use of some helpful guiding principles:

1. The more important, significant, or urgent a message, the more channels should be used.

2. When speed of transmission is the guiding factor, use informal channels. If the message is also an important one, it can be reinforced by also sending it through the slower formal channels.

3. To be authoritative, an official message must pass through formal, organization channels.

4. To be influential, the most advantageous are power and prestige channels, followed by intragroup and interpersonal channels.

5. Policies are most effectively transmitted through organization channels, but practices are more effectively transmitted through interpersonal channels.

6. A channel which ordinarily "carries" a certain type of message may "carry" other types of messages less effectively.

7. Attitudes are best reached through intragroup, interpersonal, and value channels; knowledge is best reached through the formal and ideological channels.[3]

Communication is no doubt a responsibility that leaders can never take too lightly. Speaking and listening are tools that can develop a climate of receptivity, trust, warmth, and interaction that cannot be done in any other way.

COMMUNICATION IN CHRISTIAN ORGANIZATIONS

Christian leaders often find it difficult to communicate because, first, there is the long build-up of tradition that glorifies authoritarian pronouncements: "Thus saith the Lord!" This squelches communication because people then feel they have nothing to contribute. Second, there is a tacit assumption that in Christian groups everyone shares in common the belief that we all understand each other as to the Lord's will. We therefore dislike challenging another Christian's motives or actions: we don't want to rock the boat. We may have a tendency to stifle communication so that diverging opinions will not surface.

EVALUATE YOUR COMMUNICATION

Here is a questionnaire to evaluate the communicative performance in your organization.

1. Are top management members sincerely interested in the employees, their needs, and their problems, or is top management interested exclusively in the profit picture?

2. Do members of top management make a sincere attempt to keep in touch regularly with the rank-and-file viewpoint?

3. Do the firm's employees *know* the members of top management? By name, or possibly just by sight? (This one is obviously phrased more for the big company than the small, but it could come close to home there, too.)

4. Have we (as members of management) made an effort to tell employees about our management problems, and have we ever asked for employee co-operation in solving them? Or do we handicap ourselves by the belief that employees have nothing constructive to contribute?

5. Have we made any real provision for giving our employees useful information regularly — such as bulletin boards, newsletters, face-to-face meetings, supervisory sessions, etc.? Or are we too busy being management officials to care?

6. If we *do* communicate — in short, if we answer the preceding questions with a *Yes* — do we check the effectiveness and credibility of what we do and say? Or do we simply take the employees' acceptance of the employer's veracity for granted?

7. Have we, as members of management introduced a practical, workable method by which employees can get their views to *us*? Or do we assume that we know instinctively what's on our people's minds?

8. Do our company's employees feel they belong? If the answer is Yes, just what are we doing specifically to make them feel a part of the company? If pressed, could we actually prove it?

9. Does our top management encourage employee participation in sports programs, the credit union, employee brainstorming groups, as well as political and civic activities, just to pick a few at random? Or do we pass over all this with the idea that it has no meaning?

10. Finally, a triple-headed query: Does our company have a satisfactory grievance of complaint facility? Do our people know the appropriate steps to take if the supervisor's decision — or our own — is considered unfair? Does our management actually review the "gripes" that employees make?[4]

Let us summarize why communication is so important:

1. To prepare for changes. The grapevine may beat you to it. If it does, it has usurped your prerogatives.

2. To discourage misinformation. The rumor mill specializes in misinformation because it has an active market.

3. To lessen fear and suspicion. Fear and suspicion are safer attitudes to entertain than confidence and trust. They are "safe" because the pessimist never suffers from letdowns. You must head off this incipient frame of mind, or you will have given up your right to leadership.

4. To let your people feel the pride of being well informed. The well-informed tend to become extensions of your own personality, and thus they emulate your attitudes. They must be informed on all matters that affect their psychic income. If you neglect this, your people will feel they are underpaid — in psychic income. They will then "want out." And they will not keep it secret.

5. To reduce grievances. A grievance is a personal complaint against management. It is more often imagined than real. Either way, it does the same damage, so it must be dealt with. Grievances reflect on leadership, whether justly or not.

LOOSENING THE BLOCKS TO COMMUNICATION

These are factors that hinder effective communication:

1. Do not be condescending or act like a superior judge, unless, of course, you want to choke off the source of some potentially valuable information!

2. Do not always give your opinion before your subordinates do. If you do, they will feel bound to agree with you to the limit.

3. Do not lose your control when you get bad news. The man who

does this is never volunteered bad news, so he can't deal with it effectively.

4. Do not be closed minded. Fresh facts and opinions can better prepare you to discuss and defend your position.

5. Act on other people's ideas frequently. Employees are not going to waste time pouring their creative energies into a bottomless container. Instead, they will do only what they have to do and then let the leader worry about new and better ways of doing things. The subordinates don't lose; leaders do.

This is the beginning. Let communication be your watchword. Opportunity awaits in every group for developing the kind of people who will be able to integrate out of diversity a unity of effort and purpose that enables all to achieve.

Directing Means Delegating

Delegation is the third important function necessary for good directing.

Dwight L. Moody, the famous American evangelist of another era, once said he would rather put a thousand men to work than do the work of a thousand men. When a leader can successfully fulfill this task, it saves him many frustrations. Delegating gets at the heart of directing a given group. If the leader does not delegate, he will be constantly enmeshed in a morass of secondary detail that may tear him down and prohibit him from functioning in his primary responsibilities. Someone has well said that "a man's value to his organization is measured not by what he has on his desk but what *passes over* it." This is another way of indicating how important delegation really is.

Special Problems for Christian Organizations

The world is full of dying organizations, and the Christian world is no exception. There are churches, missions, and all sorts of Christian organizations that are dying. Many of them should, because they have accomplished the task they set out to do. There was a time and place for them. They ultimately became absorbed with their function rather than their long-range goals.

A major problem is often the Christian organization founded by an individual with above-average vision. As founder, he usually makes most of the decisions; the organization grows, and he still makes all the decisions; time moves along, but he hangs on. Consequently the organization often has not kept abreast of the times because it has not inserted dynamic, new blood. It begins to die because decision-making and assignments have not been properly delegated.

But Christian groups face other problems, too, as we point out in our World Vision "Christian Leadership Letter" (August 1974):

> There are two special problems with which many executives in Christian organizations have to deal. The first of these is the use of volunteer workers. When you delegate part of your work to a volunteer, it is especially important that you make sure (1) you believe that he can do the job, (2) you have a clear understanding as to when he is going to report back to you, and (3) you have all the backup assistance that you or he may need. By carefully spelling out what is to be delegated, and checking with the delegate to be sure that he has both the time and the know-how to do the job, much of this problem can be overcome.
>
> A second, and less obvious, problem results from that which is usually a major advantage of the Christian organization — its sense of common purpose and direction. Many times your subordinates believe that they know what's best for the organization, and instead of seeing the task that you have delegated to them as coming from you they will see it as part of the *organization's* task. With such a perception, their feedback to you and communication to you about what they are doing can easily break down. Again, this kind of problem can best be handled by clearly spelling out ahead of time what is to be done and what are the checking points along the way.

It cannot be disputed that the leader who delegates in either a Christian or non-Christian organization can do more — better and faster — than the one who tries to do most things himself. Without delegation a man is limited in strength, ability, and time.

Questions to Ask

Delegation is the transfer of work from one particular employee to another. The question naturally arises, "What work, and to whom should it be delegated?" One way to approach the issue is for the leader to make an informal survey of every piece of work that crosses his desk, by asking the following questions: "Could this be done by someone else?" "Could someone else be assigned a part of the job?" "What is the worst that could happen if someone else took it over?" "Assuming someone did take it over, what specifically could I tell him or do to prevent his mishandling the work?"

Perhaps the most difficult thing for a leader to overcome is the notion that he performs a given task better than anyone else. This leads to mistrust of others. Furthermore, such an attitude or opinion really betrays a deficiency in himself, because either he cannot explain a job to another person, or he lacks the organizational skill to distribute the work properly and still oversee it through to completion.

I believe, on the other hand, it should be said that leaders should not leave all decisions to their associates. To provide the individual or the group with greater freedom than they are ready for at any given time may well tend to generate anxieties. This inhibits rather than facilitates reaching desired objectives. But this should not keep the manager from making a continuing effort to confront his subordinates with the challenge of the freedom which effective delegation brings.

THINK, THINK DELEGATION

Leaders must learn the act of delegation if they are to be effective in their leadership. How often it has been said by employees, "I have the responsibility, but not the authority." This can lead only to frustration and loss of incentive for the person who finds himself in this bind. Delegation is easy to write or talk about, but far more difficult to practice. One writer has pointed out that perhaps the best way to know if you are successful at delegating is to examine closely what happens in your office a few days before you leave on vacation.

The failure to delegate may at times be legitimate because of the deficiencies of your subordinates. If this is so, you ought to consider replacing them. Or, failure to delegate may be due to your personal insecurity. Again, if you are unwilling to make the effort to delegate responsibility, a short visit to the local cemetery may have an astounding effect!

The wise leader does not do those things that can readily be assigned to others. Not only will he develop people by delegation, but he will remain the creative person who is not dominated by unnecessary detail.

I am little impressed when I see a manager whipping himself up into a storm of activity. It's when he triggers such actions on the part of his subordinates that he earns my admiration.

An executive achieves results mainly through his people. But there's a catch. Before expecting your people to produce results, you must first qualify them to produce results.

"No executive just grows — he delegates himself into growth," a consultant once said. I couldn't agree more. Tests show that in delegating work, it is wise to transfer the job itself and not necessarily the procedure.

In the final analysis, it is the results that count. A baseball player's batting stance isn't that important — not if he manages to hit the ball fairly consistently.

Andrew Carnegie once explained his formula for success as follows: "It is very simple. I am merely a man who knows how to enlist in his service better men than himself."

Delegation carries with it four basic ideas:

1. Transfer of work
   An assigned task goes from the leader to a subordinate, and the subordinate accepts the delegated work on the basis of the expected results.

2. Transfer of authority
   This is essential in most cases. Most experts in management and organization feel that authority should be commensurate with the nature of the work.

3. Acceptance of responsibility
   If delegation is to be effective, the subordinate must be genuinely willing to perform the work and must have the initiative to get it done.

4. Importance of follow-up and accountability
   Delegation does not mean abandoning all interest in the work. The leader is still accountable, and therefore he should always be available and ready to give the subordinate help or advice if and when he needs it.

BENEFITS OF DELEGATION

Delegation always offers substantial benefits to the entire organization because it helps to develop talent and latent abilities. Let us note a few benefits:

1. Improved understanding between levels
   It seldom fails that when persons on one level undertake the work on a higher level, understanding is increased because a deeper appreciation of the problems and demands is developed.

2. Improved leader-follower relationships
   The increased understanding develops rapport, which tends to strengthen the relationship. Leaders will learn to rely more on their subordinates, and these in turn will learn how they can be more helpful to their supervisors.

3. Increased job satisfaction and morale
   Delegation is a powerful means for job satisfaction. It has been pretty well established that morale depends less on pay and benefits than on how people feel about their leaders and their work. When relationships are rewarding, people are more productive. This helps to develop a strong team spirit between departments that is vital for organizational efficiency.

BENEFITS TO THE LEADER

1. Eased job pressures
   It relieves work pressure. Holding a leadership position involves many frustrations and tensions.

2. Increased time for broader functions

By delegating less important aspects of his job, the leader frees himself for more important managerial and leadership functions. This gives him more time for planning and making careful decisions.

3. Increased chances of promotion
   This is possible because when a person delegates, it frees him to develop other skills that increase his worth to the organization. Moreover, when he is ready to assume a more responsible position, a replacement for him will be available in his department.

Benefits to Subordinates

1. Challenge and interest
   Most of our associates like a challenge, especially if they want to advance in the organization. Delegated authority gives them the chance to show what they can do, to test themselves in new situations, and to make mistakes and learn from them.

2. Increased motivation
   The opportunities provided by delegation stimulate subordinates to more effective work. If they find they are successful at tasks outside their routine, their confidence and efforts to perform and to achieve will increase.

3. Increased opportunities
   Delegation provides opportunities for subordinates to practice managerial skills, to understand the problems, pressures, and point of view of the leader and to get a broader perspective of the whole picture. In short, it prepares them both to act more responsibly in their work and to accept a more responsible position in the future.

Why Some Leaders Fail

Failure to delegate can undermine one's leadership. There are several reasons why supervisors disregard this important function.

1. They believe the subordinates won't be able to handle the assignment.

2. They fear competition from subordinates.

3. They are afraid of losing recognition.

4. They are fearful their weaknesses will be exposed.

5. They feel they won't have the time to turn over the work and provide the necessary training.

Realistically analyzed, each of these reasons points up psychological or supervisory shortcomings that actually underscore the need for delegation to help cure the ailment involved.

How to Delegate

Consider six main principles of delegation. Adhering to these will greatly enhance your own position and recognition.

1. Select the jobs to be delegated, and get them organized for turnover.
2. Pick the proper person for the job.
3. Prepare and motivate the delegatee for his assignment.
4. Hand over the work, and make sure it is fully understood.
5. Encourage independence.
6. Maintain supervisory control—never relinquish the reins.

Never forget that effective delegation aids progress, builds morale, inspires initiative. "The final test of a leader," said Walter Lippman, "is that he leaves behind him in other men the conviction and will to carry on."

You can do this through effective delegation.

Delegation is a tool seldom used well. My colleague R. Alec Mackenzie, in his book *The Time Trap,* points out the critical barriers to effective delegation:

Barriers in the Delegator

1. Preference for operating
2. Demand that everyone "know all the details"
3. "I can do it better myself" fallacy
4. Lack of experience in the job or in delegating
5. Insecurity
6. Fear of being disliked
7. Refusal to allow mistakes
8. Lack of confidence in subordinates
9. Perfectionism, leading to overcontrol
10. Lack of organizational skill in balancing workloads
11. Failure to delegate authority commensurate with responsibility
12. Uncertainty over tasks and inability to explain
13. Disinclination to develop subordinates
14. Failure to establish effective controls and to follow up

Barriers in the Delegatee

1. Lack of experience
2. Lack of competence

3. Avoidance of responsibility
4. Overdependence on the boss
5. Disorganization
6. Overload of work
7. Immersion in trivia

BARRIERS IN THE SITUATION

1. One-man-show policy
2. No toleration of mistakes
3. Criticality of decisions
4. Urgency, leaving no time to explain (crisis management)
5. Confusion in responsibilities and authority
6. Understaffing[5]

DO YOU NEED TO DELEGATE MORE?

The following are some questions to assist you toward good delegation.

1. Do you have to take work home almost every night?   Yes   No
   Why? _____

   _____

   _____

   Outline actions you can take to cut this down_____

   _____

   _____

2. Do you work longer hours than those you supervise or than is usual for hourly workers in the business?   Yes   No
   Steps you can take to change this to a No answer _____

   _____

   _____

3. Do you have little time for appointments, recreation, study, civic work, etc.?   Yes   No
   Time could be obtained by _____

   _____

   _____

4. Do you need two or more telephones to keep up with the job?
   Yes   No
   How did this come about? _____

Plans for doing something about it _____

5. Are you frequently interrupted because others come to you with questions or for advice or decisions?   Yes   No
Why does this happen? _____

Strategies for cutting down these interruptions _____

6. Do your employees feel they should not make work decisions themselves, but bring all problems to you?   Yes   No
Examples _____

To change this situation you can _____

7. Do you spend some of your working time doing things for others which they could do for themselves?   Yes   No
Examples _____

Actions you might take to avoid this _____

8. Do you have unfinished jobs accumulating, or difficulty meeting deadlines?   Yes   No
Examples _____

The jobs could be finished in time by _____

9. Do you spend more of your time working on details than on planning and supervising?   Yes   No
Why? _____

_____

_____

For a better balance you can_____

_____

10. Do you feel you must keep close tabs on the details if someone is to do a job right?   Yes   No
Examples _____

_____

_____

11. Do you work at details because you enjoy them, although someone else could do them well enough?   Yes   No
Such as_____

_____

What to do about this _____

_____

12. Are you inclined to keep a finger in everything that is going on?
Yes   No
Examples _____

_____

_____

Procedures to try instead_____

_____

13. Do you lack confidence in your workers' ability so that you are afraid to risk letting them take over more details?   Yes   No
Examples _____

_____

_____

14. Are you too involved with details (a perfectionist) that are not important for the main objectives of your position?   Yes   No
Examples _____

_____

_____

New plans to try for this_____

_____

15. Do you keep job details secret from workers, so one of them will not be able to displace you?   Yes   No
Examples _____

_____

_____

New plans for action_____

_____

16. Do you believe an executive should be rushed in order to justify his salary?   Yes   No
Why? _____

_____

_____

An executive's principal job is_____

_____

17. Do you hesitate to admit that you need help to keep on top of your job?
   Yes   No
Examples of help you can use _____

_____

List subordinates who can be trained to give this help_____

_____

_____

18. Do you neglect to ask workers for their ideas about problems that arise in their work?   Yes   No
Examples _____

_____

_____

To change this you can_____

_____

_____

What Needs to Be Delegated?

Now that you realize you should delegate more, the next logical question is, ''What should I delegate?'' We do well to remember that work to be delegated should be selected so that the benefits will be shared by both the leader and the subordinate.

First, routine details should be delegated. Minor decisions need to be referred on so the leader can concentrate on more important functions. Time-consuming tasks may also be turned over to subordinates. What seems a dull chore to the leader may be an interesting opportunity for the subordinate.

Second, when the leader is not fully qualified in a given area, the work should be handled by someone else. This is especially true when a department is highly technical or specialized. The boss may not always be up on the latest details because of new developments: his original education and training may be obsolete, or his work pressures may interfere with the time he would need to learn new skills and specialities. Tasks of this sort certainly should be delegated.

Third, delegation should take place to prevent overspecialization. If the leader becomes bogged down with the technical aspect of his work, he should consider others to help. There may come a time in a person's life when he should cease relying on his technical competence and turn his attention to developing more fully his administrative and interpersonal skills and abilities. Delegation will permit more time to increase his overall competence as a manager-leader.

Fourth, problem-solving tasks should often be delegated. Such tasks increase the decision-making skills of the subordinate and maximize his usefulness to the organization. Moreover, they add variety and challenge to his work and therefore increase his interest in it.

What Not to Delegate

Certain key functions should never be turned over to others. One reason for delegation is to free the leader so he may perform his key functions. They may be shared, but never completely delegated. Examples of this are (1) setting objectives—for the division or department for which he is responsible; (2) building teamwork—by organizing the work for maximizing coordination, communication, and cooperation; (3) coaching and developing subordinates—to acquire knowledge and skill and to increase motivation and job satisfaction; (4) setting individual goals—on quantity, quality, costs, and time.

Disciplinary matters also should never be delegated. Final authority in such matters must rest with the leader, because ultimate review of possible disciplinary action will be his anyway.

To Whom to Delegate

A leader should be flexible in his selection of individuals for delegation. There are several factors to look for in selecting people for delegation: (1) The person who seeks additional responsibility. The person who wants the chance to develop himself and to show what he can do should be provided such an opportunity; (2) The man whose potential is unknown. He may be new in the department, or someone whose job is extremely simple and routine. Delegation may give the leader a chance to evaluate better the man's performance and potential; (3) The man closest to the work. It is best not to delegate to someone several levels below, because the work will be discharged more effectively by someone closer to the actual work situation.

To Whom Not to Delegate

Certain patterns and kinds of people should be avoided: (1) Individuals outside the group. This is always resented because it is an unwarranted interference with someone else's sphere of authority and responsibility; (2) Individuals several levels below the leader. We stated this above but reemphasize it. Such delegations break the chain of effective organization. It is always best for delegation to come directly from a person's immediate superior; (3) Personal factors. This includes such subordinates who are not technically or administratively ready for added responsibility. They may not have yet mastered their own jobs, for they may not have the experience required to make them competent to deal with some of the added burdens. Furthermore, the subordinates may not be emotionally prepared; they may have doubts about their abilities, or may be satisfied and not wish to move ahead. Careful coaching sometimes is necessary before an individual is psychologically ready.

Finally, if added work is going to cut into a man's time with the regular job, his leaders should be sure the person understands this and is willing to accept it. Forcing off-hour work on subordinates without compensation for it is unlikely to lead to good morale and effective performance;

(4) Avoid favoritism. A strong word of caution is in order here, because delegating exclusively to trained and willing individuals may lead to overloading the willing worker, which could possibly have negative effects on his motivation or health; or create jealousy of a few "favorites," with resulting ill-effects on the morale of the group.

Personal Relationships in Delegation

A sound relationship is essential between the leader and his subordinates if the organization is to reap the benefits of effective delegation. There are at least five strong points to be remembered in helping to develop the proper climate for delegation which will help to get the maximum value from the process.

The *first* is trust and confidence. The subordinate must feel his supervisor is genuinely interested in delegating for the man's individual benefit as well as for his own. Trust will be built in if the following tips are maintained: (1) Do not make a man's decisions for him. Theodore Roosevelt once said that the best executive is one who has sense enough to pick good men to do what he wants done and self-restraint enough to keep from meddling with them while they do it. If for any reason the supervisor has to step in, he should explain why and make a decision in consultation with the man; (2) Do not hold back required information. To do so makes a sham of delegation; (3) Do not "breathe down a subordinate's neck" either directly or through the observations of other subordinates. This always creates uneasiness, suspicion, distrust, and resentment and can defeat the whole purpose of delegation.

Second, there should be a clear statement of accountability. This is best done in writing before the subordinate undertakes the job so that he will know precisely what results are expected. This requirement involves several considerations: (1) Make it a challenge. While making himself clear, the supervisor should at the same time avoid making the assignment sound routine or dull. Though not omitting any feature of it, he should stress those aspects that are interesting, developmental, and stimulating; (2) Objectives should be stated clearly. They must be specific, understandable, acceptable, attainable, and measurable; (3) Set clear limits. A delegated task should never be vaguely stated; the subordinate should know exactly what he is expected to do and what he should *not* do. Also, when delegating to different people, there should never be overlapping assignments. Each person should be fully aware where his assignment leaves off and his associate's begins. Setting boundaries helps people to feel more secure in accepting the delegated task; (4) Establish schedules and standards. Time limits should be clearly specified at the outset. The subordinate must understand the quality requirements governing the performance of the task. This guides him in carrying out the responsibility.

Third, a proper degree of authority should accompany the task. This may be discussed in the following ways: (1) The degree of authority must be carefully specified. Nothing can lead to greater confusion than not knowing how far one can go and what resources he can command in performing a delegated task; (2) Specifying degrees of authority. This is a suggested useful code for measuring and recording the authority associated with any delegated task or assignment:

a. Complete authority. The individual is empowered to decide and take action without consulting his supervisor beforehand or reporting to him afterward on what action was taken. This action is rarely encountered, because almost everything a supervisor does is reflected or summarized in various reports.

b. Act and report. The individual can decide and act as his judgment dictates, but must afterward report and keep his leader informed. These reports may be made either on a regular, periodic basis or as immediate, special reports.

c. Act after approval. The individual can take action only after he has consulted with the supervisor and has obtained his prior approval.

At all times, the proper degree of authority should be granted so that the person can effectively perform the delegated assignment or task.

Fourth, there should be adequate freedom to perform. Only if the subordinate is allowed to perform the delegated task will he be able to derive benefits from the delegation and truly relieve his superior of the day-to-day burden of the responsibility. This freedom should be reflected in at least two general areas. The first is freedom from close supervision. Excessively close supervision of the person's performance negates the potential benefits of the delegation both to him and to the supervisor. If the delegation is to be effective, the subordinate must be free to exercise his own judgment and perform the work in his own way. Second is freedom to make "minimum cost" mistakes. In the performance of less important tasks, mistakes are not usually very costly in terms of money or time. It is only through taking action on the basis of their own judgment, making occasional mistakes, and examining the reasons and causes of their failures that men learn how to make fewer and less costly errors and improve their decision-making ability.

Fifth, there should be adequate follow-up and feedback on results. As previously stated, overly close supervision creates distrust, ·but on the other hand the supervisor should not abandon the individual to perform strictly on his own without any form of guidance or control. Again, this may be reflected in the following ways: (1) Be available for consultation. The supervisor should be ready to counsel if and when he is asked. He should refrain from making certain decisions, but he may be able to supply additional information, guidance, and suggestions to help the subordinate make a better decision for himself; (2) Require regular reporting on results. Even though no immediate needs exist to consult with the supervisor, some arrangement for systematic reports on progress and problems is best, particularly if the delegated task covers a long time span. It should be agreed how frequently to make these reports, and the frequency may be changed if need be. Regular feedback helps to give a sense of progress and accomplishment to the project and prevents the supervisor from abdicating his ultimate accountability for the task.

Specific Techniques and Procedures

There is no sure-fire formula to cover every delegated situation, because it is a dynamic and creative process, not learned by rote. However, there are general rules that apply to most delegation situations. The supervisor should know these rules and use them intelligently, modifying them when conditions require it. Here is at least a partial list:

First, there are "don'ts" of delegation by the supervisor: (1) Don't wait until you're "snowed under" before delegating. When one is excessively busy, he cannot think through what he wants to delegate, select the right person, give adequate instructions on the task to be done, or follow up properly on performance; (2) Don't expect perfection. One cannot expect excellent performance overnight; (3) Don't be a back-seat driver. Give the needed amount of freedom and authority to go with the given assignment; (4) Don't wait until a catastrophe occurs. If the subordinate is having trouble, don't wait until things explode before stepping in. There is a fine line between back-seat driving and stepping in when it is necessary: use your best judgment to avoid the one, yet be ready to do the other.

Second is the importance of the supervisor's attitudes. From the beginning, effective delegation depends on the supervisor's frame of mind and attitude. Often the first thing he must do is overcome his own hesitation and reluctance to delegate work. There are several reasons for his reluctance, and being aware of them can help him to deal with them constructively and effectively. He may feel he can perform the task better himself; he is used to doing it, and he knows how it should be done. He may get upset and then impatient while the delegatee is learning and perhaps performing poorly. However, people learn by doing, and in time the subordinate will undoubtedly be able to perform the task satisfactorily. Again, lack of confidence in his people — because the leader may feel they are not ready, willing, or able to take on added work — can be a problem. Yet this is really a criticism that can be directed toward the supervisor. This may be a strong indication that he himself has not been doing an adequate job of selecting, coaching, and developing his subordinates. Third, the leader may not be able to communicate effectively. If this is the case, the supervisor should develop and practice these skills to aid in the delegating process.

Another problem may be the leader's desire to retain authority. This can be a real barrier when the leader is psychologically unable to share any authority with his subordinates. Such an attitude is admittedly difficult to overcome, but no manager can achieve his full potential if he has it. A basic reexamination of his own interests, abilities, aspirations, and potential may be called for to redress an imbalance between his own feelings of self-confidence and worth and the threat he feels from the superior performance of his subordinates.

Third, there must be an on-going interest in delegation. It is a two-way process, but the manager must initiate it. If he is an effective communicator, he will have a number of channels established between himself and his subordinates, and he can use these to focus the attention of his people on work that could be delegated, to stimulate their interest in undertaking them. Examples of such channels are regular group meetings (sales, production, quality, costs); performance-review interviews; weekly reports and consultation; and coaching and counseling situations.

A sound supervisor-subordinate relationship is the only framework within which effective delegation can take place. If this relationship exists, the supervisor will know the individual's interests and potential, he will have his confidence, and he will be in constant communication with him. In such a situation, an employee and his supervisor are ready for the delegation process, and they can practice it for the benefit of themselves and the entire organization.

HELPFUL HINTS

I make one final suggestion on delegating. It is wise to maintain a private "delegation performance chart." This will make you aware of those to whom you can entrust work, and you can score your own delegation successes.

In leadership it is vital to develop a balanced lifestyle. Outside interests and relaxation are needed to round out the whole personality. Delegation can actually assist your growth as a person: it will provide more time for work, play, love, and worship. This is a good prescription for executive health. Unless the leader enjoys good health and peace of mind, he cannot be on the job and working well to keep his desk cleared for action. His organization then suffers along with him.

DIRECTION MEANS DECISION

After staffing, communication, and delegation, the fourth function needed for proper direction is good decision-making. This is a major hallmark of effective leadership. Many times it is synonymous with problem-solving. There are several steps each leader should consider to enhance his ability in the process. He must first identify and describe the situation accurately; he must gain all the facts at his disposal. Second, he must line up the alternatives. All options must be considered; these may range from no action (a decision in itself) to a host of possibilities. Third, he must compare the various options; this is best done by considering both the advantages and disadvantages. Fourth, he must then consider the risks involved in each alternative. Last, he must select the best option on the basis of his total assessment.

Consider the Timing and Obstacles

When the aforementioned process is complete, the next consideration is, "When shall I proceed?" Maybe it is best to postpone until the right set of circumstances prevails. Before making the decision, it is always best to take a little time before announcing it—sleep on it first. God may have other plans.

After the decision is made, don't second-guess yourself. Commit yourself to it and motivate others who will be involved in the work. And don't seek popularity in decision-making, because leadership can often be lonely, risky, and costly. Don't vacillate. People are quick to detect it when this happens, and this can create much insecurity in an organization.

Many stumbling blocks lie in the path of effective decision-making. A serious one is a reluctance to proceed for fear of making an error. All successful enterprises in history have involved great risks; the effective leader must be willing to make mistakes and profit from them. How true the old proverb, "Not failure, but low aim, is crime."

There must be caution to assure objectivity. Decisions should be based on verified data. Economics in the use of talent and funds must be considered, and one has to be careful that he is not carried away on a wave of emotion. Perhaps the single most important consideration for the leader as he prepares to make a decision is the question, "What is the real problem?" When this is identified, the best possible solutions will be disclosed, from which the best choice will be made.

Examine the decisions a leader makes and you see accurately reflected there his ability to reason, his powers of observation, and his attitude toward people. These decisions will demonstrate whether he is positive, logical, and forward-looking, or uncertain, confused, and defensive.

Some Important Guidelines

Like other management skills, decision-making has been analyzed in great depth in recent years. Consulting firms, seminars, books, and articles point out the serious nature of this skill. Many lists have been compiled to help leaders make decisions. They can all be extremely valuable, but here is a general list that I have found useful:

1. Don't make decisions under stress. It's better to delay a decision than to make it when you're angry, upset, or under great pressure.

2. Don't make snap decisions. The spur-of-the-moment decisions are merely guesses unless they are backed up by adequate data.

3. Don't drag your feet. The decision must be made sometime. Putting it off usually results in adding to an already overflowing inventory of unfinished business.

4. Consult other people, particularly those who will be affected by your decision.

5. Don't try to anticipate everything. You'll never have all the facts, so you'll have to base your actions on those facts available at the time a decision is required.

6. Don't be afraid of making a wrong decision. No one is omniscient. There is risk involved in every decision.

7. Once the decision is made, go on to something else. You gain nothing by worrying about past decisions and you lose the capacity to give your full and dispassionate attention to other important decisions.[6]

Coordinating or directing is a continuing process. It must be maintained as well as achieved.

Notes

[1]Frank Goble, "Excellence in Leadership" (New York: American Management Association, 1972), p. 26.

[2]Ordway Tead, *The Art of Leadership* (New York: McGraw-Hill Book Company, Inc., 1963), p. 34.

[3]Lee O. Thayer, *Administrative Communication* (Homewood, Ill.: Richard D. Irwin, Inc., 1961), pp. 254-55.

[4]Ted W. Engstrom and R. Alec Mackenzie, *Managing Your Time* (Grand Rapids: Zondervan Publishing House, 1974), pp. 131-32.

[5]R. Alec Mackenzie, *The Time Trap* (New York: Amacom, 1972), pp. 133-34.

[6]Harold Shapp, "Trained Men," in *Executive's Digest*, vol. 44, no. 3 (March 1965).

CHAPTER SIXTEEN

A Leader Must Effectively Control the Operation

Necessary control is the only way the results achieved will conform to plans previously made.

Besides the major tasks of planning, organizing, and directing, the leader must perform activities designed to insure that the results achieved conform to plans previously made and approved. This he does by controlling.

We must recognize that when we delegate or direct, we do not need to lose control. When authority is delegated with a task, we don't abdicate ultimate responsibility for the work. In most cases, controls are built into the assignment itself, such as deadlines, periodic progress reports, or a prescribed budget. Controls can be few or many, but we should never hinder a task by not checking it periodically.

Several factors influence the effectiveness of controls. We can best understand this by comparing the truly professional leader with the amateur or inexperienced one: (1) The professional continually uses his mistakes as a basis for improving his future performance. The amateur may take pride in his triumph and gloss over errors; (2) The professional is systematic, not only in his personal activities, but in scheduling and controlling the work of other people and the facilities at his disposal; (3) The professional usually has a better sense of timing in making things ''jell'' in his department; (4) The professional knows how to use information to improve operations.

These characteristics require both training and experience to develop fully. But the rate at which a leader learns them can be accelerated through orderly, rational, and conscious attention to technique and method in performing all management functions. To obtain the desired results, the leader must concentrate on having plans, organization, and direction culminate in controls.

LEARNING FROM MISTAKES

Learning by trial and error can be a costly education, not only to the leader, but to his organization and to the employees in his department. The most effective way to learn is, naturally, from the experience of others, thus avoiding the errors which they have committed. Even here, however, the final touch has not been achieved, since no one ever learns the full lessons of someone else's errors. A manager who learns lessons from his own experience is apt to grow and develop faster.

The most successful method of analysis to hedge against error involves four basic steps. First, the leader must develop his plan and set performance standards. After a plan is put into operation, the results are reviewed against these standards; the differences are fed back into the planning for the second phase: performing the operations. This puts the plan into motion, directing the various phases in a way to keep them attuned to one another. Then comes the review, which measures the actual results by our holding them up against the plan or standard and noting the differences. This is supplemented by analysis of the reasons for the differences.

Finally, feedback is necessary. This brings accurate information about variations between actual and planned, and an understanding of why variances exist. Then corrective action can be taken, consisting of either changing the plan or modifying the operations.

This simple control can be used to tell what is happening or what has occurred in the past. It minimizes errors and allows a breakthrough to new and higher levels of performance.

Perhaps the worst application of this concept of control is where it is allowed to become a vehicle for the exercise of veto power on the part of a leader over any kind of positive stimulus for improvement. In such a system, the leader uses control over the communication system as a means of gaining personal power. Unfortunately, in many organizations, ideas flow upward and vetoes flow downward.

For control to be a constructive and creative force, the leader himself must serve more than a controlling administrative role. As we have noted, the leader must be a positive, driving force for innovation. No leader has produced anything by simply reading reports. The emphasis must be on performance and then controlling, rather than the reverse. A sure identifying sign of administrative stagnation is a system of unnecessarily tight controls that strangle the flow of new ideas and innovation essential for the continued growth of the enterprise.

The drive to achieve is so vital when we analyze success that we have devoted an entire chapter to this important subject. The leader must first himself be motivated. Then one of his primary tasks is to motivate his subordinates. A good help for a detailed study of this topic is the hierarchy of psychological needs introduced by Abraham Maslow, the father of modern motivation theory. His "hierarchy" is the starting point for any deep understanding of industrial motivation. The base of this hierarchy includes our psychological needs; up the ladder are our needs for safety and security, for belonging and love, then for esteem; at the top is our need for self-actualization.

Most psychologists agree today that achievement (drive, motivation, energy, ambition) is more the result of education than a genetic force or an environmental condition. People who may come out of an extremely poor background can become highly motivated. Fringe benefits, pay, job security, and working conditions do not always tell the whole story. When people are encouraged through personal growth, achievement, recognition, responsibility, advancement, and work that is interesting, then the productivity level invariably increases. When a person views his work as worthwhile, enjoyable, and exciting, he has a high sense of accomplishment.

Executives and other leaders who want to increase their effectiveness must spend time motivating people. There are useful motivating techniques which the good leader will appropriate to move his people from one point to another. A partial list of effective techniques includes goal-setting, recognition, approval, opportunity, financial incentives, freedom.

I cannot emphasize too strongly that motivation has to begin at the top. The leader must be personally interested in his people. When he is, through his own enthusiastic example people will be moved from inside themselves.

Such diagnosis will guarantee breakthroughs, but it takes more than just simple control. When a leader truly assesses his own people and motivates them — and learns from his mistakes — he is not preventing change, but improving by it.

The Professional Leader Is Systematic

The most effective leaders approach management problems by identifying areas where controls can be fruitfully applied. There are at least six basic ways in which a leader can determine when and where controls are needed, and which ones. In an orderly fashion, he studies operations to find new areas for systematizing operations.

(1) Costs as an indicator. In both profit and nonprofit organizations, the germinal nature of cost control and cost reduction is vital. In the hospital, the government agency, the religious agency, or the business firm, controlling costs is an essential first skill. Cost is a universal measuring instrument that responds to management improvement. This does not mean that a narrow-minded attention to penny-pinching is necessarily a quality of good management. It means the manager knows that his economic management is measured by his skill in distributing scarce resources among the multiple demands for them.

This kind of control through systematic analysis is not done with a meat axe. It requires that all the operations of the business or organization be weighed as alternative uses of available resources, and the best among them be chosen on a rational basis over those less suitable.

(2) Elimination of bottlenecks. In any organization there are key stations, employees, or activities that control the volume and quality of the work or activity. To the degree that the leader can modify, change, or eliminate the influence of the bottlenecks, he increases his control over the situation.

A key problem in control is the ability to find the bottlenecks and either eliminate or work around them, thus lessening their influence over the total results. The one machine, the one occupation, the one operation that produces at a lower rate than all those supplying work to it, or receiving work from it, is a bottleneck. Often leaders achieve greater productivity from a department simply through identifying this bottleneck early and, through adroit planning, circumventing its strong influence.

(3) Ability to estimate time. In developing and improving controls, the professional is often the man who has eliminated the tyranny of time over his results. He has found that estimated times required for specific chores or operations simply are not reasonable and has reduced the time estimate through rearrangement of other factors. One leader found he was spending four to five hours a day in meetings or committees. A careful analysis of his attendance at meetings and membership on committees showed him that many could be eliminated through other means of communication, and he was able to develop his own time-saver.

In work simplification it is necessary to ask of each operation, "What is its purpose?" (in order to eliminate it entirely wherever

possible). Other questions asked include —
  When should it be done?
  How should it be done?
  Who should do it?
  Could we eliminate, combine, change the sequence, simplify?
  The end product of these is better time management.

(4) Perceiving a drift in the wrong direction. A characteristic of the professional leader is his ability to establish standards that indicate clearly changes, imperceptible to casual inspection, that have taken place or are under way. Often in the day-to-day pressures of doing the job, the high standards set from the start are allowed to drift slowly but certainly downward.

This means that a systematic — perhaps continuous — review against the original standards is called for. One such method of controlling is to establish continual feedback. Under such a plan the principle of the wall thermostat is applied to social situations — variances automatically trigger responses back in the adjustment phase to correct the deviation.

In one plant, for example, the simple problem of controlling work-glove expense is handled by the foreman through an exchange system at the tool crib. When a glove is worn through, it may be exchanged for a new one; those without a worn-out glove to turn in are required to obtain a signed slip from the foreman. Thus all exceptions to his rule "no gloves supplied unless the old ones are worn out" are automatically identified by the system. Only the exceptions are brought to his attention, which actually increases his control over glove issuance; at the same time, his personal attention is not required to maintain such control.

Periodic reviews of actual results against original standards are also required where continuous control and review is either impossible or not economically feasible. Such methods as budgetary control, audits, inventories, and similar programs provide periodic reviews and checks against any losses or lapses that might not be apparent to the casual observer or noticed in routine supervision on the job.

(5) Observing changes in outside conditions. The professional leader not only establishes internal controls, but notes major shifts in the outside environment that have a bearing on the control of his department. In our day we have seen many major style changes in management practices grow out of changes in the labor market. The hard-nosed manager of the thirties discovered that new styles of motivation involving gentler modes of human relations were required when World War II came along and eliminated the labor surplus upon which his autocratic-management style had been founded. Many

discovered this change in environment only after their best employees had quit and taken jobs elsewhere or had joined a militant labor union.

Since the 1950s, many manufacturing supervisors have discovered that the need for increased productivity to avert inflation has demanded a firmer line in discipline and standards of performance than they used during the wartime conditions. This ability to adapt to his environment is characteristic of the professional in any field. His control methods reflect more than his own theories and past experience; they reflect the needs of the present-day world and the value systems by which his organization operates.

Changes in technology have affected management methods. The manager who resists new methods, or new technology with the computer, often finds that his standards can still be met but that outside changes have made them obsolete. In the automobile industry, for example, the higher horsepower of cars and the higher warranty limits granted car-buyers have imposed new quality standards that have a substantial effect on supervisory methods inside the plant. The professional is alert to such changes, and he leads his own organization in keeping abreast of the changes needed to survive and grow.

(6) Ability to see when new approaches and methods are needed. Often to the professional leader, the fact that things are being done the same way they were months or even years ago may be a sign that the whole approach needs study. This does not mean he is against stability, nor that he desires change for its own sake. At the same time, he recognizes that improvement cannot occur without change. He suspects stagnation more as a sign of weakness than of strength. Thus he systematically reviews all aspects of the organization's performance, and he regularly questions what appears to be the most staid and stable systems.

When he finds that the reasoning behind the present system remains as best, he has the wisdom not to change it. On the other hand, when he discovers that archaic methods are still being used, he plans an orderly program for eliminating or improving them.

THE PROFESSIONAL LEADER DEVELOPS HIS TIMING

A good way to facilitate direction and control is in developing timing and using available information skillfully. This ability made the small car a sound innovation, opened new markets, and pushed one kind of product into prominence over another. Lack of timing, moreover, caused the collapse of the turret-back-window Studebaker and Edsel automobiles. The American public simply was not ready for these cars; perhaps they were too far ahead of their time in style.

Managerial timing means three things principally:

(1) Master the fundamentals. The leader who most often miscalculates his timing is the fellow who forgot one of the key ingredients or who missed a fundamental fact of life. More than simply acting as a walking encyclopedia of information about his department, the wise leader adds the special creative touch that comes through the timely use of that know-how. He sees new and adroit combinations of the facts; he draws upon his experience and applies knowledge from unrelated fields to new situations.

Such a mastery of fundamentals takes time to acquire, and it means the kind of experience that time and mistakes provide. For the professional who shows good timing, the mistakes of trial and error or inexperience are behind, and the poise of the expert are evident. In addition there comes the polish of the profession when the manager continues to think creatively about his job.

From this kind of mature reflection come timing and professionalism — ingredients of the manager's job that come only to those who continue to think and dream once they can perform the minimum requirements of the job without error or hesitation.

How then are timing and professionalism developed when you are controlling? Simply by your continuing to question, inquire, and reflect about your job after you think you know all there is to know about it.

Coolness under pressure — a common companion to good timing — is also a product of this mastery of fundamentals. The supervisor who meets crises with deftness and icy nerve not only has learned all the fine details of his job, but has gone beyond this to think about the possible kinds of responses required under such situations in advance of their happening.

(2) Know the people involved. Ideas that do not get accepted, or plans that get snarled in resistance to change, are often described as being "timed wrongly." This breaks down into attitudes on the part of people who set up resistances, who find objections, or who fail to perform as expected. Good timing in managerial action demands the control of a number of human factors.

Predicting what people will do in a given circumstance is the first step. This can most often be done well by basing such predictions on knowledge of what people have done under similar circumstances in the past. Behavior tends to fall into habitual patterns, and although it is not sure-fire, it is the safest basis upon which to predict future responses.

Never forget that changing people's behavior is often a matter of just timing the change to new conditions, or of relating the changes to some significant reasons for changing. One plant manager in the Midwest discovered this truth when he took over from a retired predecessor who had permitted some rather lax habits in shop management. The employees habitually overstayed coffee breaks; wash-up time was unduly long. The new leader, not wanting to disrupt things, did not move right away to let people know what he expected of them.

After six months of continued operation under the old order, he suddenly moved to change the situation. Naturally he met considerable resistance. "Looking back on the trouble I've had," he reported, "if I had to time my moves differently, I'd be a fair but firm 'new broom' considerably sooner. When I was new on the job, I now see, I could have made the needed changes when the group actually expected some tightening. Now it looks like a hard struggle."

Working on people's habits, not their responsibilities, when introducing new ways of doing things is a sound rule for making changes. In changing timing, it is often wise to work on a group's bad habits one at a time.

Knowing that people expect consistency is another key to effective timing in leadership. The leader who tries to do two mutually inconsistent things at the same time will confront resistance to one or both changes.

Giving an idea time to "soak" is sound strategy in timing moves that involve people. Because of the habitual nature of human behavior, it may take some time for people to become accustomed to the new before they will set aside the old completely. In any group, a new idea will be eagerly sought out and accepted by a few at one extreme; at the other extreme, a few will resist all change to the bitter end.

The majority will accept change cautiously when they see the reasons for it or can see that it is beneficial or inescapable. For this group, time to see the usefulness or benefit of an idea is frequently helpful. This timing permits the internal structure of the group to accommodate itself to the new idea and makes possible the development of an informal, voluntary, cooperative pattern of behavior inside the group itself. Such a growth of coordination permits a relaxing of controls.

(3) Use logic over emotion. The leader who hopes to make controls work must avoid overemotional responses. At the same time, he will anticipate the emotional impact of change and innovation upon individuals affected.

A certain leader made some serious managerial errors and ended up with a costly strike on his hands. There were several jobs in his plant where he was losing money because of runaway incentive rates.

He was advised to take each job one at a time — to analyze and re-engineer it; in that way he could gradually reduce costs without causing insecurity and hostility. Instead, under the heat of stress, he called the union in and announced drastic changes. A long strike resulted. If he had been tactful and used logic rather than emotion, he would have spaced out his changes over a short period of time and prevented the vast losses that resulted from the strike.

THE PROFESSIONAL LEADER
USES INFORMATION SKILLFULLY

Lastly, the effectiveness of controls is determined by the leader's skillful use of a wide range of data that is both specific and general.

(1) He knows the organizational environment. The effective leader understands the general rules and regulations of the organization that employs him. He understands the prevailing organization chart (and the way things *really* operate) and how his activity fits into this. He knows the general objectives of the organization and is constantly relating his own responsibilities to those goals.

He not only is aware of the written regulations, but also knows the customs, accepted practices, and procedures of the informal organization. He knows where the centers of influence and power are, and he adapts his behavior to use them effectively. He keeps tabs on past practices and tries to use the prevailing modes of decision-making and problem-solving as far as possible.

(2) He knows the value system. Every leader who would effectively control those for whom he is responsible knows the prevailing value system of the business, organization, or ministry. He notes what gets most management attention and relates his responsibility to meeting those stated and implied goals. For example, if his organization is oriented toward production or quality without regard to costs, as might be the case with certain vital defense contractors, he has a different set of values than in a highly competitive firm where costs and quantity are the dominant values.

If he works in a pharmaceutical firm, he knows that quality and integrity of the product take precedence over costs or speed of production. If he works in a plant where toxic or explosive products are made, he knows the value placed upon safety. As a Christian he will be especially sensitive to morality and ethics in all areas of his life; his Christian value system will be evident in all his attitudes and work habits.

Since each organization has such a value environment, the leader finds that his own success is related to his ability to bring his personnel and responsibilities into line with those values. Often the personal idiosyncracies of his supervisor are part of that value system. If this person, for example, is interested in maintaining a stable and high-morale work force, the subordinate supervisor governs his practices to achieve that goal. Generally the supervisor has the responsibility of helping his immediate superior succeed and "look good," and the orientation toward that goal is sound adaptation to the value system of his organization.

When all is said and done, developing and improving controls require both technical and human skills. They cannot be achieved simply through being a good "human relator" or by being mechanically proficient in procedures and methods. They require that the supervisor have some plans and standards against which he measures his own unit's performance.

Planning, organizing, directing, and controlling—these are the essential tasks of all leaders in every field. Regardless of the style you may use in leadership, these four responsibilities cannot be minimized. Whether you're a thinker or doer, outgoing or introspective, analytical or intuitive, a conciliator or a dogmatist, good results will occur only when strong concentration and effort is made to accomplish the four managerial tasks we have considered in the last three chapters.

CHAPTER SEVENTEEN

Guidelines for Excellent Leadership

It is not so much what a leader thinks he is trying to do, but what the led are thinking.

To achieve a high quality of performance, certain ingredients must be present in a leader.

The army sergeant who says "Do what I say, not what I do" is never respected; his leadership is rejected by his men. Esprit de corps is manifest only where a leader's example is evident. Confidence, honesty, and integrity go far toward providing the best example.

If a leader does not believe in himself, no one else will. Confidence must permeate the group, and it has to proceed first from the leaders. At every stage, there must be a steady build-up of assurance, a conviction of competence based on training and gradual accumulation of experience and skill.

Furthermore, if a person doesn't feel confident himself that he can handle the next job higher up, he will never be able to sell others on his ability to handle it. Such confidence is gained only by study, application, and putting forth the best efforts day in and day out.

INTEGRITY

As a person moves up in an organization, the trail he leaves behind — both inside and outside the firm or ministry — is the critical factor in his chances for greater success. Two qualities — virtually one — that people look for in leadership (imperative in Christian leadership) are honesty and integrity.

It is useless at this point to quibble over how honest and full of integrity we and our friends *think* we are. Many an honest person has seemed to be dishonest simply because he has been careless about certain details that may raise suspicions. Therefore he suffers just as much as if he were guilty of deliberate deception. So the trail he has left behind has already been interpreted by others as they have seen fit.

Happy is the man who makes certain that this trail does not have confusing or misleading patterns that may look crooked to others regardless of how they may appear to him. The counsel of Jesus is so important: "Let your communication be, Yea, yea; Nay, nay" (Matt. 5:37). So it is not only what the person may feel about himself as to his honesty, but how others read him. What higher management wants is a man in whom others respect the authority of character. A person's trail must already have spoken loud and clear to all whom he is expected to lead and influence.

A common fallacy abounds today that to make money or be successful in the secular world, one has to compromise integrity. True, many dishonest people are successful, at least financially. But a close study of excellent leadership reveals that honesty and integrity are basic.

Subordinates can easily detect dishonest measures or questionable ethics. Following the path of least resistance, such practices usually filter down from the top and begin to permeate the whole organization.

People, to be led, must have a basic trust in their leader. They must feel they are secure in his hands because he is utterly reliable and trustworthy. Integrity becomes evident when a person displays a consistency of motives and is integrated in character and conduct.

The leader cannot afford to offend in any blatant way the standards, mores, or morals of people if he wants or expects loyalty. The acquiring of this quality is no small thing — it is a major problem that touches upon the whole of a leader's philosophy of life. There is no substitute for this kind of example.

EMPHASIZE THE FUTURE

Another major guideline for excellence is the need for a leader to look to the future. One of the leader's greatest responsibilities is to develop and train men. Excellence requires that he make men responsible by giving them tasks and providing motivation so they can achieve them in the future. To accomplish these goals the leader must do the following:

1. He must get to know his people — their abilities, their skills — in order that he may motivate them.

2. He must involve them in the planning of the organization so that their goals become the company's goals.

3. He must pass on to all of his associates the benefits they will receive as their performance increases.

4. He must learn the magic of motivation and realize that each man is motivated to a different degree for different purposes.

5. He must provide challenging leadership that brings out the best in the organization.

6. He must guide his people toward the achievement of their goal and not just their task.

7. He must remove all obstacles that stand in the way of the individuals and the unit reaching their goals and objectives.

8. He must develop an effective program of communication so that morale is increased and all personnel feel a part of the team.

9. He must lead all of his men to have achieving experiences and improve their work capacity and production on a sustained basis.[1]

DEAL WITH CAUSES

The proper handling of troublesome situations demands both tact and the ability to handle people. This requires taking the action needed to deal with basic reasons behind stress and conflict. Problems with people will not become large if you keep them little ones. To do that you must act quickly and directly when the slightest tension begins to surface between individuals.

Tact may be defined as intuitive perception. It is insight and decorum that is fit and proper in a given situation that helps to avoid giving offense. For example, a tactful person is able to reconcile two opposing views without compromising his own principles. Tact means that a person has a sensitivity to other people; whereas others might wound or hurt, he is able to use the same words or approach with a slightly different emphasis or phrasing that does not offend.

Staff problems perpetually confront the leader. We could not adequately refer to excellence in leadership without speaking to the need for handling staff conflicts.

It is obvious that in management we will have problems — let us not be surprised when they come! I am convinced that 95 percent of all our problems are personnel problems — the human equation. Not primarily equipment, methods, or even budgets — but people.

I will discuss this subject in two aspects — problems with individuals, and problems of the staff corporately. I suggest that the following qualities are needed in dealing with individuals:

1. Accessibility. Be readily available. Don't delay confronting the problem the individual brings to you.

2. Give a sympathetic hearing — even though you may not be in agreement.

3. Let every person you deal with know that you recognize his human dignity. These are people as well as employees.

4. It may well be that we should delay judgment until all the facts are in. Don't act precipitously.

5. Exhibit genuine Christian love and concern. Pray that God may help you exhibit the fruit of the Spirit. Pray with and for the one you are working with.

6. Be prepared to take courageous action.

7. Isolate the problem. The first complaint may not be (most likely is not) the *real* problem.

8. Put the problem out where it can be seen. Perhaps draw a diagram of it—or present alternatives—on a sheet of paper.

9. Have the person or people concerned tell you what they sense the answer or solution is. After it has been met and perhaps handled to your satisfaction, get a response from them. Hear from them their understanding of the problem and solution.

10. Finally, when you promise something in solution to a problem — do it!

The matter of handling staff problems corporately in a responsible way involves the following considerations:

1. Keep your people well informed. (This is a preventative.) Don't let them learn "after the fact." The majority of our problems with people reside in lack of communication or incomplete information.

2. Let your staff know frequently that you know there will be problems — and thus you are not surprised when they arise.

3. Conduct frequent and regular staff or department meetings. (To forestall or anticipate early problem areas.) Also, it is wise to have some type of a regularly published piece internally, full of information, even if you feel most of your people already know what it contains.

4. Set up clear ground rules of operation—to be reviewed on occasion. Then give frequent reminders on these. Have them clearly stated.

5. Constantly seek ways to anticipate and head off the problems.

6. When you know or hear of a staff problem, head right into it without delay so it won't fester.

7. Allow for brainstorming and facing collectively the problem areas.

When dealing with people, a sense of justice is vital in all things. People at all levels of society have a sense of what is fair and what is not. It is virtually impossible to create motivation in people without justice; as with integrity, chances are poor that justice will be a strong factor unless it is evidenced at the top levels of management in any organization.

LEARN FROM MISTAKES

The ability to profit by one's mistakes is an important quality and can often spell the difference between mediocrity and great achievement. Thomas Edison is reported to have said, "Don't call it a mistake; call it an education," when speaking to an assistant who had just burned out a filament because he had sent too heavy an electrical charge through it. Success frequently hinges on a leader's ability not to make the same mistake twice. I cringe inwardly as I reflect on the number of horrendous mistakes I have made — in judgment, in performance; but how grateful I am for the lessons learned.

Mack R. Douglas, in *How To Succeed in Your Life's Work,* provides some valuable guidelines on this matter.

1. Say only the good about other people. Never carry gossip or slander. It destroys human relationships. Of course, the person you talk about will inevitably talk about you and become suspicious of you.

2. Practice the principle that if something good cannot be said about another person, say nothing at all. Do not allow rumors to go beyond you. Let the brook stop here. If an innocent person suffers, even though the situation is true, don't say it.

3. Give honest, sincere appreciation and give all the credit due when a person has earned it. Look for opportunities to give meaningful appreciation, and be specific.

4. Once you have made a mistake, evaluate why you made it and improve your decision-making ability so that next time you are less likely to make that specific mistake.

5. Build strong bridges of communication with all people in your organization. Let them know that you value them. Develop a sense of sincere humility. Don't be a boss, demanding people. Be a friend, leading people.

6. Be big enough to admit that you are in error and then do something about it. Correct the error.

Don't be afraid of making mistakes. The man who makes no mistakes does nothing. Don't make the same mistake twice.[2]

BE FLEXIBLE

It is important to consider both long-range and short-range results in an organization. Flexibility and openness will be necessary: the ability to make changes when they are needed. Keep reexamining the program: Is there anything that should be eliminated? Are we working on tasks of yesterday when we should be bending ourselves to the opportunities of tomorrow? If a task is inherited and not bringing results, it should be dropped and forgotten.

Every program should be conceived as temporary, expendable, or ready for expiration after a few years. The assumption should be that all programs outlive their usefulness rapidly and should be scrapped unless proven productive and necessary. About every activity we must be willing to ask, "Is this still worth doing?"

If a leader does not have the ability to roll with the punches, frustration and conflict can create such anxiety that he may lose the capacity to lead. He must have the ability to adjust, as a thermometer does to the elements. He has to realize that a new endeavor may be difficult and susceptible to collapse. He therefore has to build into his thinking the means for change or bailing it out when it snags.

INVOLVEMENT WITH PEOPLE

Involvement with people may on occasion include the ability to choose between being liked and being respected. Many people confuse the two. All normal emotional human beings have a basic drive to be liked or accepted by the peer group or someone very close. Basic insecurities lead us to feel that to be respected we must be liked.

Compared with the need to be accepted, which issues from a personality need, respect has more to do with character. Respect is gained when a person displays competence. Some leaders are not particularly liked as individuals, but are well respected for their leadership abilities and competence at getting things done and done right. Respect is far more crucial to excellence than whether or not people have a deep affection for the leader.

When a man loses respect, it is a long, uphill push to regain it, if it can be regained at all. Lose a man's liking, and it is virtually impossible to change that condition. This is so important to recognize. If a leader seeks to get everyone to like him and to win a popularity contest, his authority will most likely fade with any strong wind, because to obtain their liking he has to make compromises along the way. If, on the other hand, he aims primarily to win the group's respect, he can go as far as he wishes in winning their friendship through the normal channels of human relationships.

Excellence in leadership requires meaningful relationships with people. By virtue of the fact that a leader essentially must manage, direct, or lead people, he cannot be an isolated island if he is to be successful. A Christian leader especially must be aware of personal relationships, because the Bible frequently exhorts believers to relate and indicates how to treat others — brothers as well as enemies. The Word of God basically deals with relationships throughout. For example, in Galatians 6:1,2 we are told to "bear one another's burdens." This passage is as binding in a work situation as anywhere else.

To be burdened for others means that a leader must have more than a superficial involvement with them. Probably the most important aspect of your leadership role is the manner in which you talk to, help, and relate to people. On principle, the leaders who should be most loving, caring, understanding, and redemptive are those who understand the Cross the best, for it was at Calvary that the supreme caring spirit and love was manifested by God to this hurting world.

As we accept by faith, and identify ourselves with, the love and salvation offered by Christ, His spirit takes up His residence in our hearts. His *agape* love then is given to us, and it should create a feeling of responsibility for the well-being and welfare of others. It stimulates a desire to understand others regardless of the relationship (family, work, or social).

Psychologists teach that we as individuals need to be related to others. The normal human being has both superficial social contacts and intimate, involved relationships; but at all levels he has the capacity to let others know him as he really is. So both psychology and Christianity affirm the need for meaningful human relationships.

A leader must be able to relate to others for many reasons. First, it helps to induce change in both himself and others. Interaction heightens the discovery of true feelings and allows greater trust and support between persons. When there is strong trust, a person tends to be more open and less defensive. He doesn't have to spend time proving something. Facades can drop and be replaced with directness and honesty.

Second, relating to others helps a person develop his own personality. By opening up and revealing oneself in a meaningful way, a person comes to know himself clearly as others see him. Feedback is essential: a leader who feels he has to remain isolated to retain his "omnipotence" is really fearful and immature.

If you find it difficult to relate or to open up to people, some good therapy could prove extremely helpful. Following are several factors to work on if you want to improve your rapport with people:

1. Help the other person open up by creating a climate of trust. One

way to do this is to let the other person know what your relationship can contribute to each other.

2. Try to understand where the other person is. Real communication is not only verbalization, but feeling what the other person is feeling at the moment and accepting him fully.

3. Be a good listener. Provide the other person the freedom to speak or express himself without projecting the feeling that you are prying for information that is irrelevant.

4. Try your best to be tactful. Don't be overly curious. This is somewhat related to the previous point, but let a person reveal what he feels comfortable with at the moment. Do not barge into private areas that the person obviously does not want to discuss.

5. Always respect the rights of others — what they feel, think and express.

6. Be as nonjudgmental or noncondemnatory as possible where the person's value system may differ from yours.

7. Be honest with your feelings. People can usually tell if you are masking them, and when that happens, they will follow suit.

8. Never push a relationship. If you respect a person, you will always be considerate. Coming on too strong will often cause others to withdraw, especially if they have placed a leader on a pedestal. Allow the other persons to move freely toward you if they are so inclined; much of this has to come from them because your position might make them uncomfortable.

The leader today must be armed with every means at his disposal to facilitate the interpersonal growth of an organization. This means he must be equipped to learn as much as possible about human nature. He has to understand that the whole person is involved in group action. Traits, behavior patterns, motivation levels, and responses all play a part in the way one conducts or perceives himself in the group.

For a leader who is weak in his personality and finds it difficult to relate, there are various tools and means of assistance. Tests are available today, for anyone willing to commit the time for them, that can give understanding into people's motives and responses. This material focuses on the manner and causes of people's behavior. It reveals much about how people carry on their work and can avert much bungling.

Such material reminds the leader to keep himself up to date with conditions as they really exist. Strong psychological forces continually affect the relationship of individuals to the group and to leaders. A leader must be aware of these forces to deal wisely with any disruption of relations.

Excellence in leadership requires an awareness of what is going on. I state again that it is not so much what the leader thinks he is doing as what the led are thinking. The leader can deal with problems realistically only when he seeks to know what is happening in the minds of others and understands the behavior patterns of his subordinates.

Finally, we do well to remember Christ's words: "Whatever you wish that men would do to you, do so to them" (Matt. 7:12 RSV). Always ask yourself, "How would I like to be treated in this situation if our positions were reversed?"

Notes

[1]Mack R. Douglas, *How To Succeed in Your Life's Work* (Anderson, S.C.: Droke House Publishers, 1971), p. 50.

[2]Ibid., pp. 125-27.

CHAPTER EIGHTEEN

Marks of a Christian Leader

The Christian leader never equates mediocrity with the things of God, but is always committed to the pursuit of excellence.

This book has set forth the view that leadership can be looked at from many different angles: position, relationship, and actions. Christian leaders should possess every one of the marks of excellence noted in the previous chapter. The question then must be asked: "How does Christian leadership differ?"

Christian leadership is distinctive basically in its motivation, the why of its actions. When everything extraneous is cut away, it seems to come to this: Christian leadership is motivated by love and given over to service. It is leadership that has been subjected to the control of our Lord Jesus Christ and His example. In the best Christian leaders are expressed to the utmost all those attributes of selfless dedication, courage, decisiveness, and persuasiveness that mark great leadership.

DEMANDS THE VERY BEST

No one should be more earnest than the Christian leader in the pursuit of excellence. I have the feeling that often this is a missing note in our evangelical Christian milieu. You will agree with me that God's work demands from us the very best that we have to offer Him, but too often we come to an assignment poorly prepared, or we continue to live with sloppy work habits, or we are careless in the handling of our various Christian responsibilities.

Sometime ago when I was in South Africa, I was a guest one day at the home of Gary Player, the professional champion golfer. He is an exemplary Christian, having come to a knowledge of Christ through the ministry of Billy Graham. In his home near Johannesburg, South Africa, there hangs a plaque that says, "God loathes mediocrity. He says, 'If you're going to keep company with me, don't embarrass me.' " I like that. God does loathe mediocrity.

John W. Gardner, former secretary of health, education and welfare for the United States, wrote a book with the simple title *Excellence* and the subtitle "Can We Be Equal and Excellent Too?" (New York: Harper and Row, 1961). In this work Gardner attacked the idea that it is almost undemocratic to excel at something over our fellow men. Striving for excellence in one's work, whatever it may be, is not only the Christian's duty but a basic form of his Christian witness. It might be called a foundation of nonverbal communication that supports the verbal.

Far too often in our thinking we don't mind excellence if we can shift responsibility for it onto the Lord. We say, "The Lord has really blessed his ministry, hasn't He?" or "The Lord really gave him great gifts, didn't He?" We become suspicious if someone is praised directly for doing an outstanding job. But we should recognize the human potential and give credit for a job well done.

Melvin Lorentzen has written, "Today we must stress excellence over against mediocrity done in the name of Christ. We must determine to put our best into the arts so that when we sing a hymn about Jesus and His love, when we erect a building for the worship of God, when we stage a play about the soul's pilgrimage, we will not repel men but attract them to God."

Part of our problem in wrestling with Christian excellence may be a defective theology. Many of us find it very difficult to live with the biblical truth that God is doing it all and the parallel truth that man has been given responsibility to act, yet God has commanded him to act to accomplish His will. In believing that God is in control of everything, we have a tendency to play down man's role.

Standards Are Necessary

We cannot escape it—in Christian service we are called to excellence. We are called to set standards of excellence for ourselves and all men. In his Philippian letter, the apostle Paul said much about this; indeed, it is a treatise on excellence. In Philippians 1:10, Paul prays that we "may approve things that are excellent." God, as He speaks to us in the Scriptures, never allows the good to be the enemy of the best. "Be perfect [complete] as I am" is the standard. But where do we begin? Does the call to excellence mean excellence in everything?

In Colossians 3:17 we are admonished, "Whatever you do, in word or deed, do everything in the name of the Lord Jesus, giving thanks to God the Father through him" (RSV). No higher standard can be found. The wise man, Solomon, said in Ecclesiastes 9:10, "Whatever your hand finds to do, do it with your might" (RSV). I contend that nothing less than the pursuit of excellence can possibly please God, yet most of us must admit that there are large segments of our lives in which this is not our experience.

A Measure

Excellence assumes a standard or measuring stick. Conversely anything less than excellent Christian leadership is inferior. It assumes there is a way of doing or being something that is less than the best or less than what it could be or less than worthwhile.

This kind of leadership gives us something to aim for — a mark that will render success because God wills it.

A Goal

Second, excellence assumes an objective. It demands that we think beyond dreams and concepts; that we think of reality in terms of what can be, what ought to be. We recognize that we will not achieve excellence in everything, but we must pursue it continually.

Christian leadership demands vision. The Christian leader must have both foresight and insight. When he does, he will be able to envision the end result of the policies or methods he advocates. The great missionary pioneers were without exception men of vision: they had the capacity to look beyond the present.

Vision includes optimism and hope. No pessimist ever became a great leader. The pessimist sees a difficulty in every opportunity; the optimist sees an opportunity in every difficulty.

Vision imparts venturesomeness — the willingness to take fresh steps of faith when there is a seeming void beneath.

The Christian leader will be a man of wisdom. He will have heavenly discernment. Knowledge is gained by study, but when the Holy Spirit fills a man, He imparts the wisdom to use and apply that knowledge correctly.

Paul's prayer in Colossians 1:9 was "that you may be filled with the knowledge of his will in all spiritual wisdom and understanding." That is needed for setting goals and achieving them.

PRIORITIES

Excellence also assumes priorities. It not only involves doing one thing well, but is concerned with a choice between goals. Some goals are less worthy and less honoring to God than others, goals that fall short of what God expects us to be. It is not that there is only one right way for all men, but rather that the potential for excellence in some areas lies with all men. We are called to live lives whereby we achieve excellence in at least one aspect.

Sometime ago a young man came to our World Vision headquarters from a seminary in Indiana. He related in our chapel service that one of his professors recommended that each student become a specialist in one book of the Bible. The seminarian said, "I accepted that challenge, and I determined in my life that I was going to be a specialist in the Bible book of Ephesians." Of course, that morning he preached from the Epistle to the Ephesians. He had given himself to a thorough study of the book.

Each of us is called to exercise at least one gift to its full capacity. Have you decided what your gift or gifts are? Some have great gifts but perhaps have been too lazy to unwrap them.

A vital priority is discipline. This quality is a part of the fruit of the Spirit (Gal. 5:22). Only the disciplined person will rise to his highest powers. The leader is able to lead others only because he has conquered himself and in turn been conquered by Christ.

Many people think that if they manage themselves, they will be closed in on all sides as if in a box — bound up and unable to do anything. That image should be dispelled. Managing yourself is being a good steward of your time, talent, and treasure. It is giving proper priority to things so that the most will be accomplished for the Lord.

Self-management is so important because a lack of discipline may prevent completion of the task. The Christian is accountable for his living. A study of the parable of the talents is helpful (Matt. 25:14-30): poor performance yields little reward; God expects us to invest fruitfully what He gives us.

Self-discipline does not box us in. Rather, it frees us to accomplish more with what God has given us. It also provides us with a better feeling about ourselves because of our accomplishments.

A Christian leader is a follower! This is another priority, for the art of leadership is acquired, not only by attending lectures, reading books, or earning degrees, but by first watching another person lead in action, responding to the inspiration of his person, and emulating his example.

The Savior's challenging invitation still rings out: "Follow me and I will make you become fishers of men" (Mark 1:17 RSV). As men and women heed that invitation and follow Jesus, they begin to qualify for spiritual leadership.

This principle is also seen in the life of Paul, that dynamic leader of the early church. "I beseech you, be ye followers of me" (1 Cor. 4:16). To another church he wrote, "Brethren, be followers together of me, and mark them which walk so as ye have us for an ensample. . . . Those things, which ye have both learned, and received, and heard, and seen in me, do: and the God of peace shall be with you" (Phil. 3:17; 4:9). But the apostle never asked that he be uncritically followed, as though he were a flawless pattern. "Be followers of me," he urged; immediately he laid down an all-important limitation: "as I also am of Christ" (1 Cor. 11:1). It is a matter of following men insofar as they follow Christ.

Thus leaders have to follow, remembering "them which have the rule over you" (cf. Heb. 13:7).

A PROCESS

Fourth, excellence is a process. It is more a process than an achievement. Life is a process; management is a process. We can look at an individual or an event at a certain time in history and pronounce it excellent, but it is continually pressing on that marks the person dedicated to excellence.

Paul said, "Brethren, I do not consider that I have made it on my own; but one thing I do, forgetting what lies behind and straining forward to what lies ahead, I press on toward the goal for the prize of the upward call of God in Christ Jesus" (Phil. 3:13,14 RSV).

No leader should live under the delusion that he has finally arrived. Excellence requires constant evaluation, correction, and improvement. The process, therefore, never ends.

STYLE OF LIFE

This leads us to a fifth definition of Christian excellence. Excellence has to do with the style of life. Socrates said, "Know thyself." Marcus Aurelius centuries later said, "Control thyself." Ancient sages said, "Give thyself." Jesus said, "Deny thyself."

What is your style? What can it be? We are all different. Some men are ahead of their time, some behind. Some few are musical geniuses, most are not. Some few are great preachers. Some are conceivers of grand ideas. Others are men concerned with detail. But for each of us, excellence demands that we be true to the best that God has placed within us. Our style of life must be marked by excellence.

The Christian leader can adopt nothing less as his goal.

Each must develop his own style, but I see several characteristics as absolutely necessary for the Christian leader's style of life. First, the truly Christian leader must have the indispensable quality that sets him apart from all others — his life is given over to the Holy Spirit. All the other qualifications are desirable; this one is indispensable!

It stands clear in the Book of Acts that the leaders who significantly influenced the Christian movement were men filled with the Holy Spirit. This has been true in all the history of the church.

To be filled with the Spirit is to be controlled by the Spirit — intellect, emotions, will, and body. All become available to Him for achieving the purposes of God. Such an experience is essential for successful leadership. Remember that each of us in as full of the Spirit as we really want to be!

The committed Christian leader's will has been remolded, and he is determined to do God's will at all costs. His will is not passive, but immediately active. He is able to look into the total situation and make a decision — the right one and at the right time. Someone has said that the Christian leader has a will totally willing at all times to will the will of God.

The Spirit-filled life includes self-effacement, but not self-advertisement. In God's scale of values, humility stands very high. He has always loved to advance the humble. Such a quality should be ever growing.

Paul acknowledged in 1 Corinthians 15:9, "I am the least of the apostles, that am not meet to be called an apostle." Another time he was able to boast, "I have fought a good fight" (2 Tim. 4:7). So there is the right kind of pride, but it is always tempered by humility.

Anger is another mark needed by Christian leaders. This sounds like a strange qualification for leadership, but it is a quality present in the life of the Lord Jesus Himself. Mark 3:5 says, "[Jesus] looked around at them with anger" (RSV). Righteous wrath is no less noble than love, since they coexist in God.

Great leaders who have turned the tide in days of national and spiritual decline were men who could get angry at the injustices and abuses that dishonored God and enslaved men. It was righteous anger against the heartless slave traders that caused William Wilberforce to move heaven and earth for the emancipation of slaves.

Further, a Christian leader's style of life should include a willingness or ability to be interested in people. The spiritual leader will have a love for men and a large capacity for friendship. In the Bible, David's fearless command of men sprang from the friendships he had formed; these men of renown were ready to die for him. Paul's letters glow with the warmth of appreciation and personal affection for his fellow workers. Personal friendliness will accomplish much more than prolonged and even successful arguments. The Christian leader must have a genuine respect, a liking for people; if he does, he will look for and major on their good points.

Good human relations is so vital to success. "Plans get you into things," Will Rogers once said, "but you've got to work your way out." But how do you "work your way out" — with people, and through people? One observer of the business scene refers to people as "the portals through which men pass into positions of power and leadership."

Experience repeatedly bears out that you must really care about people to get them to perform at their best level. Industrial psychologists say, "Get to know your people." The more you do, the more they will care about you. Get to know their problems, needs, home life, special interests. If my own experience is any indicator, you will grow to enjoy this.

Misunderstandings remain misunderstandings only as long as they are kept covered. Out in the open they quickly dissolve.

We need some soul-searching on this matter: Are your people genuinely convinced that you are personally interested in their well-being? Do you judge people on their ability and performance rather than on personality traits? How often do you visit with your people on an informal, person-to-person basis? Do your people get a real "charge" out of working with your group? What kind of a friend are you to your people? Do you encourage questions when you communicate — giving the other fellow an opportunity to express his views and reactions? Do your people know how they stand with you?

A lack of interest or an unfriendly attitude are obstacles in the path of achievement and lead to all kinds of personnel problems. You mean one thing; your subordinate thinks you mean another. You fail to explain a newly announced policy; your subordinate applies his own twisted interpretation. You spell out an assignment, but you don't define the measure of authority that goes with it.

A truly friendly approach involves being aware of others, seeing how vitally important it is to get through to your people, and helping them get through to you.

MOTIVATION

This mark of excellence is so important that we have devoted a whole chapter to it. It bears repeating because the Christian leader must never forget its significance.

Excellence is not easily achieved: the first 80 percent may be rather easily achieved; the next 15 percent comes much harder; only the highly motivated person on occasion reaches 100 percent.

George Allen, coach of the Washington Redskins football team, is often quoted as saying, ''I demand of my men that they give 110 percent.'' What is he saying? That on that football field he insists his men give far more than they think they are capable of giving. We have far too many leaders who settle for 70, 80, or 90 percent. When the motivation level is low, achievement is down as well. There is always a one-to-one correlation in this respect.

Motivation will keep a person from going under when the going gets tough. A good friend, Bob Cook, worked closely with me for many years. Bob said to me one day, when I was wrestling with some problems and was about ready to give up, ''Look, Ted, it's always too soon to quit!''

I don't know where you are in life, in leadership, in your role. I don't know your frustrations, your burdens, and the mountains you've got to climb. But I know this: it's too soon to quit! Never give up. Hang in there. This is part of the pursuit of excellence. There is joy in such achievement that is an all too rare experience for most of us. One of the mysteries of living is that what is easily achieved brings little inner satisfaction. We need to think big. Motivation guarantees the stamina to conquer and achieve.

ACCOUNTABILITY

Finally, all Christian leaders must be accountable to someone else. I believe every leader needs three kinds of people with whom to identify: (1) A Timothy. Paul had his Timothy. You ought to have someone you're giving yourself away to. I have such a colleague; I've had several of them in my career and thank God for them.

(2) A Barnabas — son of encouragement. Paul during his career had Barnabas. I have a Barnabas, a retired seminary professor. I go to him continually with problems, situations, difficulties. He prays with me; he counsels with me; he holds my confidence. He's Barnabas to me. Every leader needs someone he can share with intimately.

(3) A peer group. For about eight years I have been meeting five other men for breakfast in a restaurant. It is not a prayer meeting, but we pray together. It is not a Bible study, but we refer to the Word of God together. We share with each other. There is nothing we would not do for each other. Because of our schedules, seldom are all six of us there, but always three or four, sometimes five. We are accountable to each other, for we uphold each other in many ways. I am accountable to them; they are accountable to me. A leader needs to be

a part of a peer group. How we generally as Christian leaders have missed this accountability factor.

LET US REHEARSE

Remember that we need to commit ourselves to the pursuit of excellence. Bear in mind these seven marks of excellence. Let us reiterate them. Excellence is a *measurement,* and that assumes a standard of *accountability.* Excellence demands a *goal,* and that is the willingness to take risks for others. Excellence demands *priorities,* and that's telling other people or yourself what comes first in your life. Excellence is a *process,* and that means continually checking progress. Excellence has to do with *style,* and that means deciding what gifts God has given you and how to use them. Excellence has to do with *motivation,* and that's what it's all about.

How do we respond to the goal of excellence? Sort out your goals. You can't do everything; you can't be everything; and that's all right. Of those goals you believe are essential, decide which have top priority: do those with excellence. Decide who you are, what you are; decide how God made you and what He wants you to be: do that with excellence. It was said of Jesus, "Behold, He does all things well." Let's strive for that, because the God of the average is not the God of the Bible.

As we aspire to Christian excellence, keep it in perspective. Some things are more clearly excellent than others. Paul in Philippians 1:9 says we will be able to tell how we can judge what is excellent: "It is my prayer that your love may abound more and more, with knowledge and all discernment, so that you may approve what is *excellent* and may be pure and blameless for the day of Christ, filled with the fruits of righteousness which comes through Jesus Christ, to the glory and praise of God" (RSV).

Note the purpose: the glory and praise of God. Note the goal: excellence. Note the steps to the goal: knowledge and discernment, thoroughly mixed together with abounding love. The result will be the fruits of righteousness.

James Russell Lowell expressed this well:

> Life is a leaf of paper white
> Whereon each one of us may write
> His word or two, and then comes night.
> Greatly begin! though thou have time
> But for a line, be that sublime—
> Not failure, but low aim, is crime.

A Parting Word

Amidst all leadership problems we need to understand and know that we have a great God. One day many years ago, I was wrestling with a seemingly insurmountable problem: forty people were depending on me to get them to India for a conference for thousands of young people. We were to leave the day after Christmas, but on Christmas Eve we were informed that the Indian government had canceled all our visas.

In the struggle of my heart and mind, I prayed and opened my Bible. Out of the First Epistle of John flashed a message like a neon light— just a three-word statement: "God is greater!" I prayed, "Lord, if you ever had a chance to prove that you're greater than governments and the power of men, you have an awfully good chance right now!" He wrought the miracle, and the problem was resolved. "God is greater!"

Christian leaders must ever press on to the high calling and the tasks that lie ahead. Too many of us are willing to settle for "good enough" instead of "good," and "good" instead of "excellent." Let each of us, in the responsibilities God has given us, fulfill them in such a manner that people will never equate mediocrity with the things of God.

Press on. Nothing can take the place of persistence. Talent will not. Nothing is more common than unsuccessful men with talent. Genius will not. Unrewarded genius is almost a proverb. Education will not. The world is full of educated derelicts. Persistence and determination alone are overwhelmingly powerful.

(Calvin Coolidge)

Bibliography

Bruce, A. D. *The Training of Leadership*. New York: Vantage Press, 1965.

Cribbin, James J. *Effective Managerial Leadership*. New York: American Management Association, 1972.

Douglas, Mack R. *How to Succeeed in Your Life's Work*. Anderson, S. C.: Droke House / Hallux, Inc., 1971.

Drucker, Peter. *Management: Tasks, Responsibilities, Practices*. New York: Harper & Row, 1973.

Eims, Leroy. *Be the Leader You Were Meant to Be*. Wheaton, Ill.: Victor Books, 1975.

Engstrom, Ted W., and Mackenzie, R. Alec. *Managing Your Time*. Grand Rapids: Zondervan Publishing House, 1967.

Gangel, Kenneth O. *Competent to Lead*. Chicago: Moody Press, 1974.

Gardner, John. *Excellence*. New York: Harper & Row, 1961.

Goble, Frank. *Excellence in Leadership*. New York: American Management Association, 1972.

Mackenzie, R. Alec. *The Time Trap*. New York: Amacom / American Management Association, 1972.

Sanders, J. Oswald. *Spiritual Leadership*. Chicago: Moody Press, 1967.

Tead, Ordway. *The Art of Leadership*. New York: McGraw-Hill Book Co., 1963.

Wishart, J. Kenneth. *Techniques of Leadership*. New York: Vantage Press, 1965.

Wolfe, Richard. *Man at the Top*. Wheaton, Ill.: Tyndale House Publishers, 1969.

Subject Index

Scripture Index